ORNAMENTAL
TROPICAL
SHRUBS

Amanda Jarrett

Pineapple Press, Inc.   Sarasota, Florida

THIS BOOK IS DEDICATED TO MY MUM AND DAD.

Inquiries should be addressed to:

Pineapple Press, Inc.
P.O. Box 3889
Sarasota, Florida 34230
www.pineapplepress.com

All photos by the author

Library of Congress Cataloging-in-Publication Data

Jarrett, Amanda.
   Ornamental tropical shrubs / Amanda Jarrett.
      p. cm.
   ISBN 1-56164-289-4 (alk. paper) – ISBN 1-56164-275-4 (pbk. : alk. paper)
   1. Ornamental shrubs–Tropics. 2. Tropical plants. I. Title.
   SB435.6.T76 J37 2003
   635.9'523–dc21

                                                                2002014786

First Edition
10 9 8 7 6 5 4 3 2 1

Design by Shé Heaton
Printed in China

All photos by the author

ACKNOWLEDGMENTS

Many thanks to the staff of Fairchild Tropical Gardens in Miami and the Edison-Ford Estate in Fort Myers for the use of their magnificent gardens and plants. Raymond Sands of Sands Sunset Vista Nursery in Fort Myers also aided in the search for specific flowering plants in his nursery. Tom and Linda White, owners of Zone Ten Nursery in Miami were extremely helpful and kind in granting me access to their exceptional nursery.

I would also like to thank Kathy K. Puplava, horticulturist at Balboa Park in San Diego, for her support and her expertise regarding California's tropical shrubs and the local environment. Thanks to horticulturist Rob Call from the University of Arizona Extension Office for his information about Arizona's tropical shrubs and growing conditions, and to horticulturist Michelle Costa at Hawaiian Gardens Garden Center for her help regarding the microclimates, tropical shrubs, and the unique milieu associated with Hawaii. I'd like to make special mention of horticulturist Dr. Derek Burch, who was a huge help with his vast knowledge of tropical shrubs.

Thanks to Judy Gore for the opportunity to photograph her beautiful garden. Thanks also to Louise Torri, my assistant and right hand during the numerous photo shoots in sweltering temperatures and high humidity. Sylvia Bruhn was a great partner who tagged along for fun while I hunted for shrubs along McGregor Boulevard in Fort Myers.

Special thanks go to my son, Fred, and my husband, James, for their support and love while I spent many hours typing on the computer, sorting through slides, going out on photo shoots, and being totally absorbed in my work.

CONTENTS

INTRODUCTION

I was six years old when my family moved from my native England to Libya, North Africa. Upon arriving, I was soon captivated by the vibrantly colored bougainvilleas, the polished pink oleanders, and the crimson poinsettias that grew in our garden. Although we eventually moved to more northern climes, my passion for tropical flora never waned. After many years dreaming of being surrounded by exotic blooms and hot, sultry, jasmine-scented nights, I finally moved to the subtropics of southern Florida.

When people move from temperate climates to the tropics, they are often overwhelmed by the change in climate and the unusual plants. Primroses, peonies, and poppies just don't grow here. Not only are the plants different, the seasons and soils are too. It's difficult to start gardening in the subtropics and tropics if you are not armed with information and good reference material. Native species are often touted as the best and easiest plants to grow for any area, but that limits the gardener who wants to explore the wonderful world of exotic flora.

From the jungles of Malaysia to the rainforests of South America, floral treasures abound. Plants that you never knew existed can be planted in your garden of USDA Zone 10 and higher. This includes most parts of south Florida, Southern California, a small piece of southeast Arizona, and the Hawaiian Islands.

As a visual encyclopedia, this book is designed not only to introduce you to these botanic gems, but also to provide information—for the amateur and professional alike—on how to successfully grow them. To make your gardening adventure a success, I am including the essentials on plant selection and care. You'll be able to select the appropriate plant to brighten a dull corner, accent a mailbox, cover a light pole, or add zing to a boring garden island. It is easy to get caught up in the euphoria of landscaping when there are so many gorgeous specimens to entice you, so restraint and information are essential.

Information in this book is broken down into subcategories for quick reference. Numerous lists at the back also aid in plant selection and offer advice for other landscape situations. Plants are listed alphabetically under their botanical names in the Shrub Encyclopedia section for easy reference. This is the most logical way to catalog flora since common names not only vary from region to region, but numerous plants share the same common name. To help identify your favorites, I have included the common name after each botanical name. The appendix divides the plants discussed in the book into several categories, including which require full sun, which can be grown in containers, which can tolerate drought conditions, and so on.

There's such a plethora of wonderful plants to choose from, it's often difficult to see the forest for the trees (or the hedgerow for the shrubs). This book will make shrub selection and care a pleasure instead of a laborious ordeal. Now it's easy to turn your garden into a tropical paradise.

WHAT IS A
TROPICAL SHRUB?

L et's start with *shrub*. For gardeners, a shrub is pretty much
defined by its size and usage. It's the mid-size plant between the
small plants and the trees, often used as a hedge or alone as a showy
specimen. Technically, a shrub is a multi-stemmed, woody plant that
lives year after year. However, this definition is questioned by many
authorities as too limiting. There are many non-woody (herbaceous)
plants that are considered shrubs because of their shrublike appearance. Also, there are plants that have woody crowns (where the stem
and roots join), but the stems are herbaceous. To confuse matters even
more, there are herbaceous plants that eventually become woody with
age and others that are woody in one area of the country and not in
another. To blur the definition even further, some shrubs live for only
a few years.

Some shrubs can be pruned into trees and some trees can be
trained as shrubs. Shrubs that are good candidates to train as trees
don't regrow branches from the base of the plant once the branches
have been removed. Trees may be grown as shrubs as long as they
have multiple stems instead of a single trunk.

Vining plants may also be grown as shrubs when errant branches
are pruned back. Not all vines are suitable candidates for training into
shrubs as they may be too aggressive or their stems may be too thin
and weak. Once converted, a vining plant should be able to stand on
its own without support and constant trimming.

The definition of *tropical* is a tad easier to explain. Hot, usually
humid days of 70° to 85° and sultry nights of 60° or above are considered tropical. The tropics are the area between the Tropic of Cancer
and the Tropic of Capricorn. Frost is unheard of and the climate may

be wet or dry, but warm weather is year-round. Tropical areas of the world include Malaysia, the Philippines, the South Pacific, the Hawaiian Islands, Indonesia, India, the West Indies, the Caribbean, central and northern South America, and West, Central, and East Africa. These areas are where the tropical shrubs in this book originated and still grow as natives.

The subtropics have a mild climate with the possibility of infrequent frosts. Located between the tropics and temperate regions, these areas include Southern California, southern Texas, southern Florida, a small part of southern Arizona, the Mediterranean, southern Africa, southern South America, New Zealand, and most of Australia. Tropical shrubs can grow in our subtropics—Zones 10 and 11 on the hardiness zone map—with some extra care to prepare for the occasional freeze.

The desire to grow subtropical and tropical flora is universal. Many houseplants fall into the tropical category, since they originate from frost-free environments. In fact, when tourists first visit the tropics, one of the first things they notice is that many of the plants growing outside are the same ones they grow as houseplants back home.

Solariums, greenhouses, and atriums simulate the warmer climates and allow tropical flora to be grown anywhere. Many of the plants in this book are easily grown in protected environments as long as their cultural conditions are met. So just because you live in a cool climate, it doesn't mean that all these exotic beauties are off limits.

So to answer the question fully, a tropical shrub is a plant that bears multiple stems and grows where there is no frost.

Shrub Uses in the Garden

Landscape Terms

Incorporating different shrubs together within a garden can be tricky since they vary in size, shape, and tolerances. Landscape terms, such as specimen, accent, and background, help take the guesswork out of this daunting task by specifying the jobs a certain plant is able to perform. A single shrub can accomplish many functions depending on how it is used and where it is placed. To make this book user-friendly and to narrow down your choices, I have included the following terms, their definitions, and examples.

Specimen Plants

Focal points of the garden, specimen shrubs must look good all year long. One specimen is all you need since it begs for attention. Shrubs selected as specimens have more than one feature that sets them apart from the rest. Attractive flowers, leaves, bark, or shape makes them the stars of the garden. Crepe jasmine (*Tabernaemontana divaricata*) is a fine example. It bears pure white blossoms throughout most of the year with deep green, glossy leaves, and has an attractive lateral branching pattern.

Accents

An accent plant is meant to accentuate a part of the garden, a structure, or even another plant. It draws the eye to where you want attention. A bench standing alone in the middle of the lawn gets lost in the sea of green and doesn't beckon people to sit down. A plant on either side of or behind the bench not only welcomes visitors, it invites them. Plants suitable for accents should catch the eye with a unique flower, color, shape, texture, or foliage. Tropical plants, so common to tropical areas of the United States, are often large and bold, sometimes becoming over-whelming and monotonous. To break up the monotony and add excitement, aug-ment tropicals with dracaenas and cordy-lines, for example. Their long, lean lines and attractive foliage contrast nicely with bold tropicals by adding another dimen-sion to the landscape.

Contrasting textures and shapes is another method to achieve interest. The del-icate foliage of a Ming aralia (*Polyscias fruticosa*) is highlighted when it's placed among coarse, tropical shrubs. Alternately, the drooping, arching branches of a rutty (*Ruttyruspolia*) can set off surrounding plants when its shape differs from nearby flora.

The red flowers of the jatropha stand out all year, accented below by a gardenia and ti plants.

FOUNDATION PLANTINGS

Foundation plantings anchor a house to the surrounding landscape so it doesn't appear to float in a sea of turfgrass. Shrubs selected for grow-ing around the foundation should fulfill certain requirements. Ideally, good candidates should be slow growing and well behaved. Overeager varieties that are too big for their allot-ted space must be trimmed constantly to keep them in check or they soon dwarf the home, blocking windows and entranceways. Not only do they become a maintenance nightmare, the constant prun-ing eventually ruins their natu-ral shape. Flowering shrubs suffer the most because their blossoms are constantly being

This landscape design anchors the house to the sur-rounding garden.

removed by frequent shearing.

Although many foundation plantings consist of neatly clipped plants, it isn't necessary to have everything geometrically shaped. Many plants, such as the shrimp plant (*Justicia brandegeana*) and thryallis (*Galphimia gracilus*), need pruning only twice a year to keep them in shape. Their graceful forms and profuse flowers make a natural and unfussy statement without a lot of maintenance. Refrain from using thorny plants along your driveway, path, and entrance. They can become a painful nuisance for unsuspecting guests.

Most foundation plantings are too small and extend only a few feet from the foundation, making the house look as though it is teetering on a tiny oasis of shrubbery. These gardens not only look out of proportion, they don't allow room for plants to grow and they make plant selection difficult. Make planting beds large enough so the shrubs have space to mature and don't need to flow into other parts of the garden. Set plants at least three feet from the foundation wall, farther for bountiful shrubs. This makes the design more attractive and allows you easy access to paint and maintain your home. Additionally, roots have more room to spread out without the harmful effects of the alkaline properties leaching from the concrete foundation. This is especially important if the soil is already sweet.

Planting too many shrubs around the foundation is another common mistake of professionals and amateurs alike. Homeowners want an instant look; they don't want to wait for the plants to fill in and mature. Although the initial installation looks good, it's a disaster a few years down the road. Shrubs are squished against each other or are mashed against the house, while others ramble onto the lawn and pathways. Smaller, weaker plants eventually die back, while other more aggressive plants take over. Inevitably, plants get ripped out and the foundation planting has to be redone. To avoid this costly and time-consuming experience, choose your plants with care. Note their mature width and height, then space them accordingly. Do some research beforehand and you'll get, with a little time and patience, exactly what you wanted.

BACKGROUND

Deep-green plants make an excellent background for their more colorful, conspicuous cousins. They're generally one solid color rather than variegated to show off plants in the foreground. Some may have attractive flowers but their basic form is simple and consistent with dense, leafy growth from the ground up. The height of the background depends solely on what is being placed in the foreground. Appropriate shrubs include viburnum, king's mantle (*Thunbergia erecta*), and orange jessamine (*Murraya paniculata*).

The awabuki viburnum makes a great background plant with its simple, glossy, green leaves.

SCREENS

Using plants as screens provides a remedy for numerous common landscape problems. These living barriers provide privacy, block unsightly views, buffer wind, and reduce noise. Recommended plants are fast growers, bear dense foliage, and may be pruned for a formal effect or left to grow naturally. Select shrubs of adequate height to ensure the offending object is hidden. Suitable screening plants include Surinam cherry (*Eugenia uniflora*) and firebush (*Hamelia patens*).

These strategically placed hibiscus plants screen the pool area from prying eyes.

There are two types of hedges: formal and informal. Formal ones are sheared into geometric shapes such as rectangles, squares, and circles. Informal hedges are generally pruned twice a year to keep them thick and full, but they're not sheared into shapes.

The informal look is easier to maintain and includes a wider selection of shrubs. Many flowering plants are suitable candidates since they're able to bloom to their heart's content without being threatened with shears. Generally, pruning twice a year, in spring and fall, is all they need to keep them bushy and attractive.

This schillings holly hedge accents the already formal design of this garden.

Foliage size, flowers, and growth rate are important factors when selecting shrubs for a formal hedge. Suitable shrubs bear dense growth; twiggy, leafy stems with small foliage; and inconspicuous or petite flowers. Hibiscus is often used as formal hedge material, but it grows so quickly it's difficult to keep in check. Constant pruning robs the plant of its magnificent flowers, which defeats the purpose of growing it. More appropriate candidates are yaupon holly (*Ilex vomitoria*) and orange jessamine (*Murraya paniculata*).

An informal plumbago hedge looks lovely intermingled with a wrought-iron fence.

MASS PLANTINGS

Massing, like ground-cover, is a term used to describe many plants of the same type grown in one bed. Mass plantings provide consistency of color, form, scale, and texture, usually over a large area. This common technique works well for any part of the garden, depending on the size of the plants used. Bedding plants, such as impatiens, are often massed together to form a blaze of color. It's a dramat-

A mass of plumbago brings attention to the garden and the long lines of the pine tree.

ic touch that's easily done with shrubs as well. Plants suitable for this technique should not be too tall, so they don't overwhelm the garden and surrounding plants. Consider a mass planting of cocoplum (*Chrysobalanus icaco*) under a grove of pine trees to create a natural and attractive landscape. Indian hawthorn (*Rhaphiolepis indica*), downy jasmine (*Jasminium multiflorum*), and wild coffee (*Psychotria nervosa*) are also suitable for mass plantings.

GROUPS

Grouping numerous shrubs together is an easy way to add drama to your garden. Plant three or more of the same shrub together in a cluster. The key to a good group is to use uneven numbers (three, five, seven, etc.), as the odd man out gets to go in the middle. Many shrubs are suitable for grouping as long as they have enough space to mature. For an exotic and bold look, use chenille plants (*Acalypha hispida*), or consider aralias (*Polyscias*) to create vertical columns.

One chenille plant is dramatic, but several of them are eye-catching.

SHRUB BORDERS

A shrub border is full of different kinds of shrubs and may be intermingled with perennials, bulbs, and bedding plants. The different textures, shapes, colors, and sizes of the integrated plants is as bold, eclectic, or uniform as you want it to be. To make an attractive shrub border, however, you must maintain some order and use a layering technique so the final result

Combining different heights and textures and just a few colors makes an attractive garden. This shrub border includes peach angel trumpet, dwarf fuschia bougainvillea, and blue plumbago.

doesn't look like a hodgepodge. Use taller plants—whether it's trees, palms, or large shrubs—as the garden's backbone. The next layer is the understory, which consists of medium-height plants, followed by a layer of smaller shrubs in front. The icing on the cake is the groundcover plants, bulbs, perennials, and bedding plants. A consistent massing of bedding plants or groundcovers at the feet of the taller plants ties everything together.

Although a shrub border begs for a variety of shrubs, it is wise to be selective. Mix up the textures so it doesn't become monotonous, and be thoughtful about the colors, whether it's foliage or flowers. For example, many different types of crotons, with their vibrant, rich leaves, can easily overwhelm a garden. Use them sparingly to add accent and pizzazz to the border. A good idea is to draw a plan on paper first, then place the plants, still in their pots, on the ground so you can shift them around to obtain the effect you want. Examples of appropriate border plants are yesterday-today-and-tomorrow (*Brunfelsia pauciflora*) and Brazilian plume flower (*Justicia carnea*).

BANK COVERS

Many gardens have steep slopes, which are difficult to mow and maintain. The tendency of soil to slip or erode from a bank is a major consideration when you're planning a bank cover. Plants suitable for bank covers are sprawling shrubs with tenacious roots and rooting stems that hold the soil together. Mass the same shrubs together for a pleasing and consistent effect. Since most plants suitable for covering slopes have a large spread, give them lots of room and plant accordingly. Examples include red powder puff (*Calliandra haematocephala*), downy jasmine (*Jasminium multiflorum*), and shining jasmine (*Jasminium nitidum*).

A suitable plant for a bank cover is the shining jasmine.

BUTTERFLY GARDENS

If you want butterflies in your garden, you must provide them with food for all the stages of their development from caterpillar to butterfly. Caterpillars eat foliage and stems, while butterflies sip the nectar from flowers. The adult butterfly lays her eggs close to or on a plant suitable for her babies to feed on. As the caterpillars hatch, they begin their feeding frenzy. Although the shrub may be (but is not usually) eaten to the ground, its roots are intact and bounce right back, ready for the next generation. To attract and keep butterflies in

A butterfly drinks nectar from a blue clerodendrum.

your garden, grow many different kinds of larval and nectar plants. Cassias are suitable larval plants, and red powderpuff (*Calliandra haematocephala*) attracts butterflies.

Bird Gardens

Birds need food, water, shelter, nesting material, a place to nest, and protection from predators. Shrubs with multi-branched limbs and lots of dense foliage provide a safe haven for our fine, feathered friends. Ones bearing fruit also supply them with food. Shrubs to attract birds include cocoplum (*Chrysobanus icaco*), orange jessamine (*Murraya paniculata*), and powderpuff (*Calliandia haematocephala*).

Powderpuffs are a favorite of birds.

Invasive Plants

Some invasive plants are beautiful, but they have a nasty tendency to overtake the garden with underground or aboveground runners that pop up new plants away from the mother plant. Many shrubs send up new shoots from their base, but invasive ones take it one step further, reforesting large areas in no time. The invasive umbrella tree *(Schefflera actinophylla)* is illegal to grow in some Florida counties

Viable seeds are another problem. Not every shrub that produces seed has the ability to repopulate the planet, but others do. A non-invasive shrub may have a few seeds germinate or none at all.

The umbrella tree is extremely invasive. Its seeds are eaten by birds, and seedlings pop up all over the place.

When a shrub yields both seeds and runners, it means trouble. When non-native species escape from cultivation and find their way into the native ecosystem, the consequences can be disastrous. The Brazilian pepper tree (*Schinus terebinthifolius*) is a perfect example of the havoc a non-native shrub can wreak. Over the last century in Florida, this plant has crowded out native vegetation, much to the detriment of native animals that depend upon indigenous flora for their survival. The Brazilian pepper tree is so noxious, in fact, that it is illegal to sell, possess, or grow it in Florida. Check with your local horticultural extension agency for potentially troublesome and illegal plants.

The Brazilian pepper tree is ubiquitous in Florida.

The pagoda flower (*Clerodendrum paniculatum*) and its relative the Java glory-bower (*Clerodendrum speciossisum*) are two examples of invasive shrubs that readily form colonies with their underground stems, but they're not so wild that they infiltrate the native ecosystem. For homeowners with large expanses of ground to cover, some slightly aggressive species have their place, but for the most part, these nuisances cause gardeners to throw up their hands in despair. If you do decide to plant *legal* invasives, which are not a threat to the native ecosystem, be prepared to give them lots of room or keep them container bound.

Give the invasive glory bower room to spread as it sends out babies from the base.

CONTAINERS

Most shrubs are suitable for growing in pots as long as the container is big enough to accommodate their root systems. Use sterile potting soil rather than soil from the garden, which contains pathogens and weed seeds. For a lighter mix, add one or two parts vermiculite to four or five parts potting soil. It improves the drainage and does not float to the surface like perlite and styrofoam bits. It also keeps the pots lighter so they are easier to move around. Mix in a slow-release fertilizer when preparing the soil so the plant has a steady dose of food.

For large pots, the weight and volume of soil can be cumbersome and expensive. Crushed aluminum cans or styrofoam peanuts at the bottom of these containers take up space, reducing the amount of soil and its weight.

All plants (other than bog and pond plants) must have good drainage or their roots will rot. Although it is often recommended to cover drainage holes with rocks or bits of broken clay pots, it's not necessary and it sometimes hinders drainage. For arid regions where watering is a daily chore and for plants that like moist soil, place a drainage tray underneath the container to catch the superfluous water. This gives the shrub a chance to absorb the extra water it needs. After ten minutes, throw away any excess so the roots don't become waterlogged. Another idea is to use a drip irrigation system. Adding a polymer to the soil also reduces watering by increasing the soil's moisture-holding capacity. Polymers absorb and retain moisture. When dry, they resemble small, hard crystals, but they become soft, swollen, jellylike blobs when wet. You can find drip irrigation systems and polymers wherever garden products are sold.

A medinilla is quite happy in its pot in this shady spot.

This container-grown eugenia is trained into a topiary.

17

SHRUB

ENCYCLOPEDIA

Shrubs in this section are in alphabetical order by scientific name.
Below is an index of shrubs by common name.

Chenille Plant, Love-lies-bleeding
Acalypha hispida

Origin: Indonesia   *Salt tolerance:* medium
Zone(s): 10–11   *Type:* evergreen
Drought tolerance: low   *Growth rate:* fast

Soil: tolerant of most but prefers rich, moist, and well-drained
Exposure: full sun
Size: 5' to 8' tall by 4' to 8' wide
Form: upright, bold with large, 8", green leaves; has a weeping form when in flower
Flower: long, drooping, deep-red cattails up to 18" long; flowers year-round
Fruit: not applicable
Problems: aphids, scale insects, mealybugs
Uses: specimen, accent, foundation, shrub border, containers

A showstopper when in flower. Prune after flowering to control growth and promote bushiness. *Acalypha hispida* 'Alba' bears white flowers.

Copperleaf
Acalypha wilkesiana

Origin: Pacific Islands
Salt tolerance: medium
Zone(s): 10–11
Type: evergreen
Drought tolerance: low
Growth rate: fast

Soil: tolerant of most but prefers rich and moist
Exposure: full sun
Size: 8' to 12' tall and wide
Form: wide and bushy with large, bold leaves in various shades of red and green, depending on the variety
Flower: insignificant
Fruit: not applicable
Problems: mealybugs, powdery mildew
Uses: screen, hedge, accent, shrub border, foundation

Prune in spring and fall to keep lush. Tolerates poor drainage and prefers ample moisture. Many varieties are available including 'Java White'. It has cream and green variegated foliage and grows to 12'. 'Picotee' and 'Godseffiana' have ruffled, green leaves edged in cream and grow to 8'. 'Fire Dragon' (*A. wilkesiana* 'Ceylon') has twisted, reddish green foliage with pink-beige margins and grows to 10'. 'Musaica' bears multicolored leaves with green, russet, and red markings.

'Ceylon'

'Java White'

'Picotee'

'Musaica'

Pineapple Guava
Acca (Feijoa) sellowiana

Origin: South America   *Salt tolerance:* medium
Zone(s): 9–11   *Type:* evergreen
Drought tolerance: high   *Growth rate:* medium

Soil:	prefers rich, moist, and well-drained
Exposure:	full sun to partial shade
Size:	10' to 15' tall and wide
Form:	bold, upright, round form; shiny, deep-green, leathery leaves with silvery undersides
Flower:	tufts of red stamens and four white petals on 1" flowers in spring
Fruit:	oval, gray-green fruit up to 4" long; edible and fragrant
Problems:	none
Uses:	hedge, accent, foundation, tree, specimen, shrub border

Both flowers and fruit are fragrant and edible and attract birds. Fruit is suitable for jams and jellies. When grown as a tree, its attractive, reddish, peeling bark is accentuated.

Acca (Feijoa) sellowiana

Acca (Feijoa) sellowiana
developing fruit

Bush Allamanda
Allamanda schottii

Origin: South America
Zone(s): 10–11
Drought tolerance: high

Salt tolerance: medium
Type: evergreen
Growth rate: medium

Soil: tolerant of most but prefers rich and well-drained
Exposure: full sun
Size: 5' to 10' tall by 6' to 8' wide
Form: horizontal branching pattern
Flower: 2" yellow, tubular flowers year-round
Fruit: round, spiny 1" fruit
Problems: none
Uses: shrub border, specimen, foundation, accent

Becomes spindly if not pruned annually, but otherwise an easy and attractive plant. Tolerates drought once established. Does better when planted in fertile soil. Allamanda 'Silver Dwarf Discovery' bears silver foliage, but it's not as vigorous or as hardy as the green variety.

Allamanda schottii

'Silver Dwarf Discovery'

Allamanda schottii
seed pod

Philippine Violet
Barleria cristata

Origin: India and East Indies
Zone(s): 10–11
Drought tolerance: low

Salt tolerance: low
Type: evergreen
Growth rate: fast

Soil:	tolerant of most but prefers rich loam
Exposure:	full sun to partial shade
Size:	4' to 6' tall by 2' to 3' wide
Form:	stiff, dense shrub with round, green leaves
Flower:	1" lavender, funnel-shaped flowers year-round
Fruit:	seeds held in hairy capsules
Problems:	leafspot in summer
Uses:	hedge, shrub border, accent

Grown mostly in southern Florida. Self-seeds but is not considered invasive. Cut back to keep growth compact. A white variety, which has become naturalized in southern Florida, is also available.

Barleria cristata (white form)

Barleria cristata
(purple form)

Nasturtium Bauhinia
Bauhinia galpinii

Origin: South Africa

Zone(s): 10–11

Drought tolerance: medium

Salt tolerance: low

Type: evergreen

Growth rate: medium

Soil: tolerant of most with good drainage

Exposure: full sun

Size: 5' to 9' tall by 10' to 15' wide

Form: wide, sprawling shrub that likes to climb; pale green leaves are two lobed

Flower: nasturtium-like flowers from dark red to orange in spring through autumn

Fruit: dark brown pods

Problems: none

Uses: informal hedge, vine, bank cover, massing, container, bonsai

This sprawling, vinelike plant can be trained into a shrub by pruning. Its attractive shape, leaves, and flowers, combined with its versatile growing habit, makes it a useful addition to the landscape.

Bougainvillea
Bougainvillea spectabilis

Origin: Brazil　　　　　　　　　*Salt tolerance:* high
Zone(s): 10–11　　　　　　　　*Type:* evergreen shrubby vine
Drought tolerance: high　　　　　*Growth rate:* medium

Soil: prefers dry, well-drained
Exposure: full sun
Size: 15' to 40' tall and wide
Form: sprawling with green, heart-shaped foliage and thorny stems
Flower: colorful, paperlike bracts surround off-white, star-shaped flowers in the center most of the year
Fruit: inconspicuous
Problems: caterpillars
Uses: specimen, accent, screen, shrub border, hedge, tree

This popular plant, with its spectacular clusters of flowers in fuschia, red, yellow, orange, purple, mauve, and white, is often equated with the tropics. Some varieties bear variegated leaves, such as 'Raspberry Ice', with its green and gold leaves and red blossoms. This is a very versatile vine: it can be pruned into a shrub or tree, espaliered against a wall, or grown in containers. When left to its own devices, it will cascade over walls, cover fences, and scramble up trees, making a spectacular display of color. Dwarf varieties grow only a couple of feet high and are suitable for hanging baskets and groundcovers. Needs full sun to flower well. Avoid overwatering as this hinders flowering. Since bougainvilleas are large and quite thorny, avoid planting them in areas they'll soon outgrow and near walkways, driveways, or doorways.

E *Bougainvillea spectabilis* 'Raspberry Ice'

Bougainvillea spectabilis dwarf variety

Snowbush
Breynia disticha

Origin: Pacific Islands
Zone(s): 10–11
Drought tolerance: medium

Salt tolerance: low
Type: evergreen
Growth rate: medium

Soil: tolerant of most
Exposure: full sun to partial shade
Size: 5' to 8' tall by 4' to 7' wide
Form: Loose, airy shrub with small white and green leaves. New foliage is touched with soft pink.
Flower: white in summer and autumn
Fruit: not applicable
Problems: occasionally caterpillars or mites
Uses: specimen, shrub border, foundation, hedge, tree, massing, container

Remove lower branches to grow as a tree. A beautiful but invasive plant that produces underground runners. Prune to keep growth compact to desired shape and height.

Angel Trumpet
Brugmansia species

Origin: South America

Zone: 10–11

Drought tolerance: low

Salt tolerance: low

Type: evergreen

Growth rate: fast

Soil: prefers rich and moist

Exposure: partial shade in a sheltered location

Size: to 20' depending on variety; canopy width of 15'

Form: multi-stemmed, large shrub with a broad canopy, and large, light green foliage

Flower: Trumpetlike, fragrant flowers are 8" or longer and borne profusely every few months. Colors vary from white to peach, yellow, and pink, depending on the variety.

Fruit: uncommon with most varieties

Problems: spider mites, mealybugs, tomato hornworms, nematodes, numerous viruses

Uses: specimen, tree, container, shrub border

A magnificent showpiece when in flower. Most varieties bloom profusely monthly. Blossoms are mostly fragrant in the morning and evening. All parts are poisonous if ingested.

Brugmansia versicolor

'Charles Grimaldi'

Yesterday-today-and-tomorrow
Brunfelsia pauciflora 'Floribunda'

Origin: Southern Brazil   *Salt tolerance:* medium
Zone(s): 10–11   *Type:* evergreen
Drought tolerance: medium   *Growth rate:* medium

Soil: rich, well-drained, and acidic
Exposure: full sun to partial shade
Size: 7' to10' tall by 5' to 8' wide
Form: dense habit with deep-green foliage
Flower: 1" flat, fragrant, deep-purple flowers that fade to pale violet then white from spring to summer
Fruit: not applicable
Problems: none
Uses: container, accent, shrub border, foundation

Flowers are borne in profusion, covering the plant. Prune after flowering to desired shape and height. *Brunfelsia australis* is more shade tolerant. 'Macrantha' has larger flowers than 'Floribunda'. Needs extra iron to keep the foliage green. Might sucker with new shoots that emerge from its base. All parts are poisonous if ingested.

Dwarf Poinciana, Pride of Barbados, Barbados Fence, Red Bird of Paradise
Caesalpinia pulcherrima

Origin: West Indies

Zone(s): 9–11

Drought tolerance: high

Salt tolerance: medium

Type: evergreen; deciduous in colder areas

Growth rate: fast

Soil:	tolerant of most with good drainage
Exposure:	full sun
Size:	6' to 9' tall and wide
Form:	loose, airy shrub with small green leaves
Flower:	orange and/or yellow exotic poinciana-like flowers in spring, summer, and autumn
Fruit:	long, brown seedpods
Problems:	scale insects, mushroom root rot
Uses:	screen, accent, shrub border, desert gardens

Tiny leaves on thin, willowy stems produce a delicate, fernlike appearance. Requires little water. Pods and seeds are poisonous if ingested.

Red Powderpuff
Calliandra haematocephala

Origin: Bolivia

Zone(s): 9–11

Drought tolerance: high

Salt tolerance: low

Type: evergreen

Growth rate: fast

Soil:	tolerant of most
Exposure:	full sun
Size:	8' to 10' tall by 10' wide
Form:	sprawling, airy, wide shrub with fernlike, green foliage
Flower:	red, 2" to 3" pompomlike, fragrant flowers most of the year; flower buds resemble ripe raspberries
Fruit:	small seeds in flat pods
Problems:	scale insects, mealybugs, thornbugs
Uses:	background, screen, specimen, accent, bank cover, hedge, massing, bird and butterfly gardens

A beautiful plant for its form, flowers, and attractive raspberry-like flower buds. Prune to desired shape and height. 'Nana' is a dwarf variety that grows to only 5' by 4' and flowers most of the year. *Calliandra emarginata* is a dwarf species that grows to 4' by 6' and bears cherry-pink flowers. Flowers provide nectar for adult butterflies and attract hummingbirds.

Natal Plum
Carissa grandiflora

Origin: South Africa

Zone(s): 10–11

Drought tolerance: high

Salt tolerance: high

Type: evergreen

Growth rate: fast

Soil: tolerant of most

Exposure: sun to partial shade

Size: 6' to 10' tall by 4' to 8' wide

Form: dense, compact growth with deep-green, glossy, leathery leaves and thorny stems

Flower: fragrant white, flat flowers in spring, summer, and fall

Fruit: edible red berries used for preserves

Problems: none

Uses: screen, accent, background, hedge, foundation, specimen, bank cover, bonsai, container

An excellent shrub for the beach as it tolerates sandy soil, salt, and high winds. Avoid placing it near walkways because of its sharp thorns. Prune to desired shape and height. 'Fancy' is more upright with large fruit. Dwarf Natal Plum, *Carissa macrocarpa*, grows to 2' with a 4'-to-8' spread. 'Horizontalis', 'Minima', 'Prostrata', 'Tuttle', 'Green Carpet', and 'Boxwood Beauty' are other dwarf varieties. Dwarf varieties are suitable for massing and bear smaller thorns.

Carissa grandiflora   *Carissa grandiflora*   *Carissa grandiflora* fruit

Yellow Cestrum
Cestrum aurantiacum

Origin: Guatemala   *Salt tolerance:* medium
Zone(s): 10–11   *Type:* evergreen
Drought tolerance: medium   *Growth rate:* fast

Soil:	tolerant of most but prefers rich loam
Exposure:	full sun to partial shade
Size:	5' to 8' tall and wide
Form:	broad shrub with arching branches and deep-green leaves
Flower:	clusters of yellow, tubular flowers year-round
Fruit:	small, white, poisonous berries
Problems:	caterpillars
Uses:	butterfly gardens, shrub border

An attractive plant that produces large flower clusters in abundance. Attracts butterflies and hummingbirds.

Night-blooming Jessamine or Jasmine
Cestrum nocturnum

Origin: West Indies
Zone(s): 10–11
Drought tolerance: medium

Salt tolerance: medium
Type: evergreen
Growth rate: fast

Soil: tolerant of most but prefers rich loam
Exposure: full sun
Size: 8' to 12' tall by 4' to 8' wide
Form: wide-spreading, arching, branching habit with deep-green, shiny leaves
Flower: chartreuse, 1", tubular, fragrant blossoms in profuse clusters that open at night throughout the year
Fruit: occasional small, white, poisonous berries
Problems: caterpillars sometimes are a severe problem
Uses: fragrance gardens, shrub border

Prune back severely after flowering to prevent lankiness. Give it plenty of space. Avoid placing it where its scent could become overpowering.

Cocoplum
Chrysobalanus icaco

Origin: Caribbean and Florida   *Salt tolerance:* high
Zone(s): 10–11   *Type:* evergreen
Drought tolerance: medium   *Growth rate:* medium

Soil:	tolerant of most but prefers sandy
Exposure:	full sun
Size:	10' to 20' tall by 15' wide, depending on variety
Form:	coarse, broad, dense form with deep-green, round leaves up to 3" long
Flower:	small, white clusters year-round
Fruit:	1 1/2" green fruit that matures into purple, grapelike, edible berries
Problems:	none
Uses:	beach properties, massing, shrub border, tree, foundation, hedge, container, accent, screen, background, bird gardens

An easy and attractive plant. Prune to desired shape and height. 'Red Tip' has dark red, new leaves and grows to 12' by 10' if left unpruned. 'Hobe Sound Dwarf' grows to 6' with a spread of 12'.

Chrysobalanus icaco immature fruit

'Red Tip'

Chrysobalanus icaco mature fruit

Clerodendrum
Clerodendrum

Origin: Asia, Africa, India
Zone(s): 10–11
Salt tolerance: low

Type: evergreen
Growth rate: fast

Drought tolerance: low to medium, depending on variety
Soil: tolerant of most but prefers rich loam
Exposure: full sun to partial shade
Size: depends on species
Form: large, bushy, bold, dense growth with large leaves
Flower: small flowers borne in large clusters year-round
Fruit: not applicable
Problems: none
Uses: specimen, screens, shrub border, accent plant

The Pagoda Flower, *Clerodendrum paniculatum*, grows to 6' with red flowers held in large, upright clusters. The Tube Flower, *Clerodendrum minahassae*, grows to 10' by 10' and has white tubelike flowers that flare open, followed by red seed heads that open into stars with a blue seed in the center. Blue Clerodendrum, *Clerodendrum myricoides* 'Ugandense', has two-toned blue flowers on 10' by 5' plants. The Glory Bower, *C. speciosissimum*, grows to 12' and bears clusters of scarlet flowers. Shooting Star, *Clerodendrum quadriloculare*, grows to 10' by 10' and bears large, pale pink flowers. The Cashmere Bouquet, *Clerodendrum bungei*, has clusters of fragrant pink or red flowers that attract butterflies on 5'-to-7' tall plants with large 1' leaves. *Clerodendrum bungei, C. speciosissimum, C. paniculatum,* and *C. quadriloculare* produce suckers and are considered invasive. Prune after flowering to keep compact.

Clerodendrum minahassae

Clerodendrum minahassae tube flower seed head

Clerodendrum speciosissimum

Clerodendrum quadriloculare shooting star clerodendrum

Clerodendrum myricoides
'Ugandense'

Croton
Codiaeum variegatum

Origin: Malaysia
Zone(s): 10–11
Drought tolerance: high

Salt tolerance: medium
Type: evergreen
Growth rate: slow

Soil: tolerant of most
Exposure: full sun to partial shade
Size: 3' to 8' tall by 3' to 6' wide, depending on variety
Form: broad, bold, and round
Flower: insignificant
Fruit: not applicable
Problems: scale insects, mealybugs, thrips, spider mites, rot in poorly drained soils
Uses: shrub border, accent, screen, specimen, container plant, hedge, foundation

Very colorful, bold plants so use them sparingly. Colors are generally more vibrant in full sun. Available in many shapes, sizes, and colors with leathery leaves, depending on variety. The dwarf variety, 'Mammey', grows to 5' by 4' but may be maintained at 1' by 1'. Sap may cause skin irritations and stains clothes.

Codiaeum variegatum hedge

'Jan Bier'

'Desirable'

'Miss Aceton'

Silver Buttonwood
Conocarpus erectus var. sericeus

Origin: Florida, West Indies
Zone(s): 10–11
Drought tolerance: high
Growth rate: medium
Soil: tolerant of most
Exposure: full sun
Size: 15' to 35' tall by 20' to 30' wide
Form: vase-shaped with attractive silver, velvetlike foliage
Flower: inconspicuous
Fruit: small, brown, conelike clusters
Problems: scale insects, mealybugs, sooty mold
Uses: accent, screen, shrub border, hedge, tree

Salt tolerance: high
Type: evergreen shrub or small tree

The soft, silver foliage contrasts nicely with surrounding tropical plants. When grown as a tree, its bark adds to its uniqueness as it becomes deeply ridged and twisted with age. This common Florida plant is prone to scale insects and mealybugs, which encourage black, sooty mold, discoloring the pretty foliage. Green buttonwood (*Conocarpus erectus*) grows to 40' with a 30' canopy when grown as a tree and is more cold tolerant than its silver cousin. It's also resistant to insects, therefore reducing the sooty mold. 'Silver Sheen' is a smaller, silver-leaved hybrid, which is also less susceptible to insects and diseases. Buttonwoods are great plants for inhospitable conditions, as they are tolerant of drought, wind, poor drainage, and high salinity.

Conocarpus erectus var. *sericeus* with fruit

Conocarpus erectus var. *sericeus* immature specimen as shrub

Ti Plant, Hawaiian Ti
Cordyline fruticosa (terminalis)

Origin: Eastern Asia
Zone(s): 10–11
Drought tolerance: medium

Salt tolerance: low
Type: evergreen
Growth rate: medium

Soil: tolerant of most
Exposure: partial sun to shade
Size: 3' to 15' tall by 2' to 8' wide, depending on variety
Form: upright, narrow form with red and/or green variations, depending on variety
Flower: inconspicuous on some varieties, but others bear small yellow or purplish flowers clustered along small sprays
Fruit: bright red berries
Problems: scale insects, mealybugs
Uses: accent, shrub border, foundation, container plant

An attractive vertical accent. Lower leaves fall off, leaving the stem bare with a tuft of foliage on top, adding to its long, lean lines. Plant will produce multiple branches where it is cut. The cuttings root easily in soil. Colors sometimes are more vivid in partial shade. 'Haole Girl' bears wide green and cream foliage. 'Amabilis' has pink, pale green, and cream markings. 'Iwao Shimizu' is a dwarf with green leaves edged in orange. 'Baby Ti' has green leaves edged in red and is a dwarf variety growing to 2'.

Cordyline fruticosa   'Haole Girl'   'Amabilis'

Madagascar Rubber Vine, Rubber Vine
Cryptostegia madagascariensis

Origin: Madagascar

Zone(s): 10–11

Drought tolerance: high

Salt tolerance: medium

Type: evergreen to semievergreen vine or shrub

Growth rate: medium

Soil:	rich, moist, well-drained
Exposure:	full sun
Size:	5' to 10' tall and wide if pruned
Form:	horizontal shape when grown as a shrub with shiny, thick, deep-green leaves
Flower:	lilac, bell-shaped flowers in summer and autumn
Fruit:	large, green, pod-shaped twin capsules
Problems:	scale insects
Uses:	accent, vine

The beautiful, mauve flowers contrast magnificently with the deep-green, shiny foliage. Although it's considered a vigorous vine, reaching 60', it becomes an attractive shrub when pruned. Seeds are viable, so remove them before they mature. The rubber vine is aptly named as it bleeds a milky substance known as latex, which may cause skin irritations. It sometimes becomes deciduous in the winter in subtropical areas. The Palay Rubber Vine, *Cryptostegia grandiflora*, is a little better behaved and grows to 7' if pruned.

Cryptostegia madagascariensis grown as shrub

Cryptostegia madagascariensis flowers

Horn of Plenty, Devil's Trumpet
Datura species

Origin: China

Zone(s): 10–11

Drought tolerance: low

Salt tolerance: low

Type: evergreen, shrubby perennial

Growth rate: fast

Soil:	rich, moist, and well-drained
Exposure:	partial shade
Size:	4' to 5' tall and wide
Form:	coarse with thin, green leaves
Flower:	yellow, white, or white with purple, 8", trumpet-shaped, fragrant flowers with single, double, or triple petals year-round
Fruit:	1" round capsules full of seeds
Problems:	nematodes, spider mites
Uses:	specimen, container, accent

Although the Datura is technically a perennial, its shrubby nature and exotic blossoms bear mention. The purple flowering varieties (*Datura metel*) are white on one side and purple on the other. Their stems are also a deep, shiny purple. *Datura metel* 'Aurea' is a yellow variety. Seeds are viable and can be invasive. A short-lived plant that lasts only a few years. All parts are poisonous if ingested.

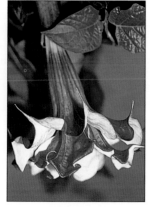  

Datura metel flore pleno   *Datura metel flore pleno* seed head   'Aurea'

Hydrangea Tree, Tropical Snowball, Pink Ball, Mexican Rose
Dombeya species

Origin: Africa, Madagascar, and Mascarene Islands

Zone(s): 9–11

Drought tolerance: low

Salt tolerance: low

Type: evergreen

Growth rate: fast

Soil:	tolerant of most but prefers rich loam
Exposure:	full sun
Size:	can grow up to 30' in Hawaii but usually grows to 10' elsewhere
Form:	multiple-stemmed shrubs with broad canopies, and green, bold, slightly hairy leaves up to 12" long
Flower:	3" to 8" round clusters composed of many pink flowers from summer through fall
Fruit:	not applicable
Problems:	aphids, scale insects, nematodes
Uses:	tree, specimen, shrub border, container

All of the many species are magnificent when in flower, resembling pink hydrangeas. Rosemount (*Dombeya x* 'Rosemount') grows to 10' with a dense, mounded crown. Pink Ball (*Dombeya wallichii*) is a tall species growing from 20' to 30' with a 20' to 25' canopy. The spent, brown flower clusters persist on the plant and look unsightly. Keep soil moist after planting until the plant is established. Sensitive to drought.

'Rosemount'

Dombeya x cayeuxii

Dombeya x cayeuxii

Dracaena
Dracaena

Origin: tropics
Zone(s): 10–11
Drought tolerance: depends on
          species

Salt tolerance: depends on
          species
Type: evergreen
Growth rate: slow

Soil:	tolerant of most
Exposure:	partial sun to shade
Size:	4' to 15', depending on species
Form:	narrow, vertical form with multiple trunks and linear leaves of numerous colors, depending on variety
Flower:	depends on variety but grown mostly for attractive foliage
Fruit:	not applicable
Problems:	occasional leaf spot diseases
Uses:	containers, shrub border, foundation, accent, lanai

Many dracaenas lose their lower leaves, accenting their lean stems, which may twist and turn, depending on variety (*D. marginata, D. reflexa*). *Dracaena marginata* (Red-edged Dracaena) grows to 8' to 15' by 4' to 8' and bears narrow green leaves edged with a red stripe. The Corn Plant, *D. fragrans* 'Massangeana', grows from 5' to 10' by 2' to 5' and bears wide, ribbonlike leaves with a yellow stripe down the center. It bears pleasantly scented flowers year-round. The Dragon Tree, *D. draco*, reaches 30' by 20' and has a stout trunk topped with clusters of 2', sword-shaped leaves. The Ribbon Plant, *D. sanderana*, bears slender stems with white and green striped foliage and grows to 4' by 2'. Reflexed Dracaena, *D. reflexa*, bears short, twisted leaves and grows to 8 to 15' by 6' to10'. A variegated variety is the Song of India (formerly *Pleomele reflexa* 'Variegata'). *Dracaena deremensis* 'Janet Craig' is 6' to 10' tall by 3' to 6' wide and has dark green, arching leaves. 'Warneckii' has white and green striped foliage. Many other dracaenas, including dwarfs, are also available.

Dracaena sanderana

'Tricolor'

'Bicolor'

Dracaena reflexa
'Song of India'

'Warneckii'

Dracena marginata
Red-Edged Dracaena

Golden Dewdrop, Pigeon Berry, Sky Flower
Duranta erecta

Origin: Caribbean

Zone(s): 9–11

Drought tolerance: high

Salt tolerance: medium

Type: evergreen

Growth rate: medium

Soil:	tolerant of most
Exposure:	sun to partial shade
Size:	8' to 15' tall and wide
Form:	broad shrub with arching branches, simple green leaves, and small but sharp barbs at the base
Flower:	fragrant, 1/2" flowers in loose clusters from spring through autumn; colors include pale blue, white, purple, and purple with a white frill
Fruit:	showy but poisonous 1/4" orange-yellow berries
Problems:	scale insects, nematodes
Uses:	screen, hedge, background, foundation, shrub border, accent, container, bird and butterfly gardens

Very showy when in flower. Easy to prune to desired height and shape. Numerous varieties available including a variegated yellow and green form (*D. erecta* 'Golden Edge') and a green and white variegated variety (*D. erecta* 'Variegata'), as well as the white golden dewdrop (*D. erecta* 'Alba'). Flowers are larval food for butterflies and attract hummingbirds. The plant is toxic to cattle, and the berries are poisonous if ingested by humans.

Duranta erecta   fruit   'Variegata'

Blue Sage
Eranthemum pulchellum

Origin: India

Zone(s): 10–11

Drought tolerance: low

Salt tolerance: medium

Type: evergreen

Growth rate: fast

Soil: tolerant of most but prefers moist, and well-drained

Exposure: partial shade to shade

Size: 4' to 6' tall by 4' wide

Form: round

Flower: clusters of blue flowers from autumn through spring

Fruit: not applicable

Problems: scale insects

Uses: massing, container, accent, foundation

Very attractive plant with lush leaves and pure blue flowers. Cut back after flowering to keep compact.

Surinam Cherry
Eugenia uniflora

Origin: Brazil
Zone(s): 10–11
Drought tolerance: medium

Salt tolerance: medium
Type: evergreen
Growth rate: medium

Soil: tolerant of most but prefers rich and well drained
Exposure: full sun to partial shade
Size: 8' to 20' tall by 6' to 15' wide
Form: multiple stems are tan with thin, peeling bark and glossy, oval, 2", aromatic leaves
Flower: 1/2", fragrant white flowers in spring
Fruit: red, cherry-sized, ribbed, edible fruit
Problems: scale insects
Uses: hedge, bird gardens, screen, background, tree, foundation

Easy to prune to desired height. Remove lower branches to train as a tree to reveal its attractive bark. Birds love the fruit and dense growth for protection and nesting. The edible fruit is spicy and tart and is suitable for making preserves. Considered invasive as seeds germinate readily.

Eugenia uniflora hedge

fruit

Eugenia uniflora

Poinsettia
Euphorbia pulcherrima

Origin: Mexico, Central America
Zone(s): 10–11
Drought tolerance: low

Salt tolerance: low
Type: evergreen
Growth rate: fast

Soil: rich, moist, and well-drained
Exposure: full sun
Size: 8' to 10' tall by 4' to 6' wide
Form: upright with thin, green leaves
Flower: small, beadlike flowers are surrounded by colorful bracts in winter
Fruit: not applicable
Problems: whiteflies, mealybugs, spider mites, caterpillars, root rot, poinsettia scab
Uses: container, shrub border, accent, houseplant

Must have complete darkness at night to initiate flowering for Christmas, so avoid planting near a porch light or streetlight. Tends to get spindly and sparse, so cut back by one-third at Mother's Day, Memorial Day, and again in July. Don't prune after Labor Day or the flowers won't be ready for Christmas. Many varieties available, including the traditional red, yellow, pink, marbled, and double flowering forms. Milky sap may irritate skin and eyes.

Thryallis
Galphimia gracilis

Origin: Mexico, South America		*Salt tolerance:* medium	
Zone(s): 10–11		*Type:* evergreen	
Drought tolerance: medium		*Growth rate:* medium	

Soil: tolerant of most

Exposure: full sun

Size: 4' to 6' tall by 4' to 6' wide

Form: loose, graceful with light green, glossy leaves

Flower: bright yellow, 1", star-shaped flowers are borne in dense clusters and flower year-round

Fruit: not applicable

Problems: none

Uses: accent, foundation, hedge, massing, shrub border

An easy-care plant that needs occasional pruning to keep it compact. Stems are brittle and break easily. The Shower-of-Gold, *G. glauca*, is a taller species growing to 5' to 8' by 4' to 6'.

Gardenia
Gardenia jasminoides

Origin: China

Zone(s): 8–10

Drought tolerance: low

Salt tolerance: low

Type: evergreen

Growth rate: slow

Soil: rich, acidic, moist, and well-drained

Exposure: full sun

Size: depends on species and variety

Form: upright, stiff, round

Flower: fragrant, roselike but with a waxy texture, white to cream colored, up to 5" wide from spring to early summer

Fruit: not applicable

Problems: scale insects, nematodes, aphids, mealybugs, sooty mold, whiteflies

Uses: container, hedge, accent, bonsai, screen, background, foundation

Gardenias are known for their beautiful, sweetly scented blossoms. 'Mystery' is a common hybrid that grows from 4' to 8' with an equal spread. It bears pure white, roselike flowers commonly used in florists' corsages. 'Radicans' has prostrate growth only 6" to 2' tall by 3'. *Gardenia thunbergia* grows to 10' with single, white, 4" flowers. The Tahitian gardenia, *Gardenia taitensis*, bears single, white, highly fragrant pinwheel flowers most of the year on plants reaching 15'. Must have acidic soil or foliage becomes yellow and sickly. Needs a 3" layer of organic mulch. Use only varieties grafted onto the nematode-resistant *Gardenia thunbergia* rootstock. Prefers a north or east exposure in desert locations. Difficult to grow in alkaline soils.

Gardenia jasminoides

Gardenia jasminoides

Gardenia taitensis 'Tahitian'

Wild Cotton, Upland Cotton
Gossypium hirsutum

Origin: Florida,Central America   *Salt tolerance:* high
Zone(s): 10–11   *Type:* evergreen sub-shrub
Drought tolerance: high   *Growth rate:* fast

Soil: tolerant of most
Exposure: full sun
Size: 6' to 8' tall by 8' wide
Form: upright with many hairy, red branches and three-lobed, green leaves
Flower: white or pale yellow, hibiscus-like flowers that turn purplish pink with age
Fruit: fringed bracts surround greenish white fuzz encasing small seeds
Problems: none
Uses: tree, accent, container, shrub border, novelty plant

An attractive shrub that lives only for a few years. The seed capsules are used to make cotton. Hawaiian cotton, *Gossypium tomentosum*, grows wild in the arid, rocky regions of the Hawaiian Islands. It grows to 6', bears yellow flowers most of the year, and is often used in leis. Although it's in the cotton family, it's not used as a source of textile cotton, but the foliage is used to make green dye. Plant breeders also use the Hawaiian species to improve pest resistance for commercial cotton.

Gossypium hirsutum flower   *Gossypium hirsutum* seed head   *Gossypium hirsutum* plant

Caricature Plant
Graptophyllum pictum

Origin: New Guinea

Salt tolerance: low

Zone(s): 10–11

Type: evergreen

Drought tolerance: low

Growth rate: fast

Soil: tolerant of most but prefers moist and fertile

Exposure: full sun to shade

Size: 3' to 8' tall by 2' to 5' wide

Form: compact and full with variegated leaves up to 6" long

Flower: pinkish red, 1/2", tubular flowers borne in clusters in summer

Fruit: not applicable

Problems: aphids, mealybugs

Uses: container, accent, hedge, foundation, shrub border, screen

Grown for its colorful foliage. Leaves bear cream-colored centers edged in gold, green, or brown. 'Tricolor' has a cream center splashed with pink, surrounded by green margins. Prune to keep compact. Tolerates poor drainage and prefers moist soil.

Firebush, Scarlet Bush, Hummingbird Bush
Hamelia patens

Origin: southern Florida, Caribbean
Zone(s): 9–11
Drought tolerance: high

Salt tolerance: medium
Type: evergreen
Growth rate: fast

Soil: sandy and well-drained
Exposure: full sun to partial shade
Size: 6' to 12' tall by 5' to 8' wide
Form: wide, graceful, loose, and open with thin, simple, green leaves
Flower: 3/4", tubular, orange to red flowers in clusters year-round
Fruit: small, glossy, black berries
Problems: scale insects occasionally
Uses: screen, shrub border, background, accent, hedge, specimen, butterfly and bird gardens

An easy plant that needs room. Red leaf and flower stalks add to its charm. Attracts butterflies and birds, including hummingbirds. The Bahama Firebush, *Hamelia cuprea,* bears larger, bell-shaped, yellow flowers with orange stripes and grows to 8'. The African Firebush, *Hamelia patens* 'African', grows to 8' and bears orange flowers with red stripes.

Hamelia patens

Hamelia patens

Hamelia cuprea 'Bahama'

Hibiscus
Hibiscus rosa-sinensis

Origin: China   *Salt tolerance:* medium
Zone(s): 10–11   *Type:* evergreen
Drought tolerance: low   *Growth rate:* fast

Soil: fertile, moist, and well-drained
Exposure: full sun
Size: 7 to 12' tall by 6 to 10' wide
Form: shrubby, upright with deep-green, glossy leaves
Flower: large funnel-shaped with prominent stamens year-round
Fruit: not applicable
Problems: nutrient deficiencies in sandy soils, nematodes, whiteflies, aphids, scale insects, spider mites, leaf spots
Uses: hedge, accent, specimen, shrub border, tree, container, screen, foundation, bird and butterfly gardens

Needs rich, moist soil to perform well. Prune in spring and fall to keep compact. Benefits from a 3" layer of organic mulch to maintain soil moisture and improve soil's fertility. Many flower colors are available, including double forms. Flowers last only one or two days but are borne in profusion. Double flowering varieties tend to drop their flower buds prematurely. Some also have variegated white and green foliage. 'Red Hot' hibiscus has red and green leaves with a red blossom. 'Carnival' has green, red, and white foliage with a red flower. The Fringed Hibiscus, *Hibiscus schizopetalus,* has a weeping habit and bears lacey-fringed pendant flowers in red, white, or pink. Grows to 15' by 12'. The Confederate Rose, *Hibiscus mutabilis,* is deciduous in colder climates, with double, roselike flowers that open pink or white and change to deep red by evening. Grows to 15' by 8'. Anderson Crepe Hibiscus is commonly grown as a 12' tree. It bears single, light pink blossoms on long, pendulous, weeping stems. Flowers provide nectar for adult butterflies and attracts birds. The giant whitefly is a serious pest for hibiscus in southern California.

Hibiscus rosa-sinensis
'White Wings'

Hibiscus rosa-sinensis
'Pink Passion'

Hibiscus rosa-sinensis

Hibiscus rosa-sinensis

Hibiscus rosa-sinensis 'Matensis'

Hibiscus rosa-sinensis 'Carnival'

Hibiscus mutabilis

Hibiscus rosa-sinensis

Hibiscus schizopetalus

Hibiscus rosa-sinensis 'Scarletta'

Hibiscus rosa-sinensis

Chinese Hat Plant, Cup and Saucer, Parasol Flower
Holmskioldia sanguinea

Origin: Himalayas
Zone(s): 10–11
Drought tolerance: low

Salt tolerance: medium
Type: evergreen
Growth rate: medium

Soil:	tolerant of most
Exposure:	full sun to partial shade
Size:	6' to 10' tall by 8' wide
Form:	sprawling, wide habit
Flower:	clusters of unusual round bracts with a central, prominent stamen in orange, red, bronze, or yellow year-round
Fruit:	not applicable
Problems:	nematodes
Uses:	background, screen, bank cover, shrub border

The curious but attractive flowers resemble their numerous common names. This sprawling plant needs lots of room. Remove old canes at their base, and cut back plant to keep it compact and bushy. Peak flowering season is summer and autumn. May defoliate during drought.

Yaupon Holly
Ilex vomitoria

Origin: southeastern United States *Salt tolerance:* high
Zone(s): 7–10 *Type:* evergreen
Drought tolerance: high *Growth rate:* medium

Soil: tolerant of most
Exposure: full sun to light shade
Size: 15' to 20' tall by 10' wide
Form: compact, dense growth with 1", gray-green leaves
Flower: inconspicuous
Fruit: red or yellow 1/4" berries on female plants
Problems: none
Uses: small tree, topiary, container, foundation, shrub border, lanai, massing, hedge

An easy plant, especially for the beach, as it's drought and salt tolerant. Dwarf varieties are popular, as they are more versatile. 'Nana' has a round form and is easily maintained at 4'. If left unpruned, however, it grows to 7' with an equal spread. 'Schillings Dwarf' bears red, immature leaves. It's easily kept at 4' by 4', although it naturally grows to 7'. 'Stokes Dwarf' has purple stems and grows to 4' but is often maintained at 18" by 3'. 'Pendula' is a weeping form and is best grown as a tree. Many other *Ilex* varieties are available. Yaupon Holly forms thickets due to underground stems.

Ixora
Ixora species

Origin: southern Asia

Salt tolerance: medium

Zone(s): 10–11

Type: evergreen

Drought tolerance: medium

Growth rate: medium

Soil: rich and well-drained

Exposure: full sun

Size: 2' to 12' tall by 2' to 8' wide depending on species and variety

Form: dense, upright, twiggy with bronze, immature leaves that mature into deep green, leathery leaves

Flower: large, round clusters of tubular flowers with flat, flared petals borne in profusion year-round in red, yellow, pink, white, or orange

Fruit: red berries that turn black at maturity

Problems: scale insects, aphids, nematodes, bagworm, mushroom root rot, nutrient deficiencies

Uses: hedge, accent, foundation, massing, specimen, container

Many varieties are available. *Ixora* 'Nora Grant' grows to 6' with large, coral flower clusters and is considered nematode resistant. *Ixora* 'Maui' bears large leaves and large clusters of orange-red blossoms on 4' plants. The 'Petites' have small leaves, compact growth to 2' by 2', and orange, red, yellow, or deep-pink flowers. *Ixora casei* 'Super King' is the tallest ixora, growing to 12' by 10', and bears red flower clusters 6" across. Flame of the Woods, *Ixora coccinea*, grows to 10' by 6', with red, orange, pink, or yellow flowers. Due to their dense, twiggy growth and tolerance of frequent shearing, ixoras are often pruned into formal shapes, especially hedges. They need fertile soil, regular applications of acidifying fertilizer, and 3" of organic mulch to prevent yellow leaves and promote vigor.

Ixora casei 'Super King'

Ixora 'Maui Yellow'

Ixora 'Petite Red'

'Magee's Yellow'

Ixora 'Petite Pink'

Star Jasmine, Downy Jasmine; Shining Jasmine
Jasminium multiflorum; Jasminium nitidum

Origin: India	*Salt tolerance:* depends on species
Zone(s): 10–11	*Type:* evergreen
Drought tolerance: medium	*Growth rate:* fast

Soil: tolerant of most
Exposure: full sun to partial shade
Size: 6' to 10' tall by 4' to10' wide
Form: vining shrubs with glossy, deep-green leaves
Flower: white, starlike, fragrant, 1" flowers most of the year
Fruit: not applicable
Problems: scale insects
Uses: container, hedge, shrub border, vine, massing, bank cover

Downy, or Star, Jasmine (*J. multiflorum*) has a slight scent and downy stems. It can grow over 6' feet tall when used as a shrub and up to 15' if left as a vine. Shining Jasmine, *Jasminium nitidum*, has a similar habit and bears fragrant flowers in the summer. May be used as a vining plant to cover arbors and fences if left unpruned. Easy to prune to desired shape and height.

Jasminium nitidum

Jasminium multiflorum

Jasminium nitidum

Peregrina Jatropha
Jatropha integerrima (hastata)

Origin: Cuba

Zone(s): 10–11

Drought tolerance: high

Salt tolerance: medium

Type: evergreen

Growth rate: fast

Soil: fertile and well-drained

Exposure: full sun to partial shade

Size: 10' to15' tall by 8' wide

Form: bushy and upright with deep-green leaves that vary in shape from lobed to oval

Flower: clusters of red, 1/2" flowers with bright yellow stamens year-round

Fruit: greenish red seed capsules

Problems: scale insects, mealybugs

Uses: small tree, container, foundation, shrub border, accent, specimen, butterfly and bird gardens

A low-maintenance plant that's always in flower. Remove the lower branches to convert into a small tree. Seeds are viable but not invasive. Prune in spring by one-third to keep growth compact. Easy to prune to desired shape and height. Dwarf Peregrina, *Jatropha integerrima* 'Compacta', grows to a maximum size of 8' by 7' but is easily maintained at 4' by 3'.

Jatropha integerrima

Jatropha integerrima

Coral Plant
Jatropha multifida

Origin: Tropical America
Zone(s): 10–11
Drought tolerance: high

Salt tolerance: medium
Type: evergreen
Growth rate: medium

Soil:	tolerant of most
Exposure:	full sun
Size:	10' to 15' tall
Form:	deeply lobed leaves are lacelike and graceful
Flower:	bright red, coral-like texture produced year-round
Fruit:	chartreuse, round nuts form in center of flower cluster
Problems:	spider mites, scale insects
Uses:	accent, specimen, foundation, tree, container, shrub border

Very unusual and striking plant due to its lacey foliage and exotic flower heads. A low-maintenance plant. Seeds are poisonous if ingested.

Shrimp Plant
Justicia brandegeana

Origin: Mexico   *Salt tolerance:* low
Zone(s): 9–11   *Type:* evergreen
Drought tolerance: low   *Growth rate:* fast

Soil:	tolerant of most with good drainage
Exposure:	partial shade
Size:	3' to 4' tall and wide
Form:	graceful and slightly weeping
Flower:	blooms year-round with small, white flowers that emerge from salmon-pink bracts
Fruit:	inconspicuous
Problems:	none
Uses:	shrub borders, foundation, container, bank cover, hedge, bird gardens, houseplant, accent

An attractive shrub year-round due to its soft arching stems and ever-present flowers. Prune in spring to promote bushy growth. A chartreuse variety is also available. White Shrimp (*Justicia betonica*) grows to 5' by 4' and has white, 4" bracts with tiny, lilac flowers within. Flowers attract hummingbirds. Performs best with afternoon shade.

Justicia brandegeana

Justicia brandegeana

Justicia brandegeana

Justicia betonica

Flamingo Flower, Brazilian Plume Flower
Justicia carnea

Origin: South America
Zone(s): 10–11
Drought tolerance: low

Salt tolerance: low
Type: evergreen
Growth rate: medium

Soil:	prefers rich, moist, and well-drained
Exposure:	partial shade to shade
Size:	3' to 4' tall by 2' to 3' wide
Form:	upright, stiff
Flower:	large, bright pink plumes year-round
Fruit:	not applicable
Problems:	scale insects
Uses:	container, massing, shrub border, accent, houseplant, foundation

An attractive, well-behaved plant. Prune in spring to promote bushy growth. Avoid afternoon sun.

Justicia carnea

Crepe Myrtle
Lagerstroemia indica

Origin: southern Asia, Australia   *Salt tolerance:* low
Zone(s): 7–10   *Type:* deciduous
Drought tolerance: high   *Growth rate:* medium
Soil: fertile, moist, and well-drained
Exposure: full sun
Size: 10' to 20' tall by 15' to 20' canopy
Form: upright with broad, spreading canopy and small, green
               leaves
Flower: crepelike petals in conical clusters from late spring
               through summer in red, purple, white, or pink
Fruit: brown seed capsules
Problems: powdery mildew, root rot, aphids
Uses: accent, shrub border, specimen, tree, foundation, container

Crepe myrtles are very versatile and are easily converted into trees by removing their lower limbs, which accentuates their attractive reddish, shiny, peeling bark. Dwarf forms are also available and grow from 3' to 5', depending on the variety. To extend the flowering season, remove the spent flower heads before they set seed. After the flowering period, remove all flowers and small twiggy growth to increase flower size and production for the next year. The Queen's Crepe Myrtle, *Lagerstroemia speciosa*, is a tree growing to 35' and bears sprays up to 15" long with 5" purple flowers. Must have full sun, especially in the morning, to prevent powdery mildew. Root rot occurs with poor drainage.

Lagerstroemia indica   *Lagerstroemia indica*   *Lagerstroemia speciosa*
                                                                 Queen's Crepe Myrtle

Texas Sage, Silverleaf
Leucophyllum frutescens

Origin: Texas, Mexico
Zone(s): 8–10
Drought tolerance: high

Salt tolerance: medium
Type: evergreen
Growth rate: slow

Soil:	well-drained and sandy
Exposure:	full sun
Size:	5' to 8' tall by 4' to 6' wide
Form:	dense, spreading with soft, silver-gray foliage
Flower:	flared, lavender in summer
Fruit:	not applicable
Problems:	none
Uses:	hedge, shrub border, foundation, container, accent, desert, bird and rock gardens

Mainly grown for its attractive silver foliage. To prevent plant becoming bare at the bottom, prune the sides as well as the top. Easy to prune to desired shape and size. Suitable for desert regions as it tolerates dry conditions and heat. Birds use it for protection and nesting.

Japanese Privet, Wax-leaf Privet
Ligustrum japonicum

Origin: Japan

Zone(s): 7–10

Drought tolerance: high

Salt tolerance: medium

Type: evergreen

Growth rate: medium

Soil: tolerant of most

Exposure: full sun to partial shade

Size: 8' to 10' tall by 8' wide

Form: upright, spreading with deep-green, shiny, leathery leaves

Flower: small, white, fragrant flowers borne in clusters in late spring

Fruit: deep-purple berries

Problems: leafspot disease, leafminer, scale insects, whiteflies

Uses: specimen, hedge, screen, small tree, container, foundation, shrub border, background

Grown for its form and bold foliage. Remove lower branches to convert into a tree to reveal its attractive branching pattern. Easy to prune to desired shape and size. 'Rotundifolium' bears round, green leaves, and 'Frasieri' sports yellow and green variegated foliage. 'Jack Frost' bears white and green leaves. The Chinese Silver Privet, *Ligustrum sinense* 'Variegatum', sports small, oval, green leaves edged in white and grows to 8'. Its clusters of small, white flowers are showy and fragrant. Leafspot and leafminer are common in Florida, disfiguring the foliage.

Ligustrum japonicum

Ligustrum japonicum 'Jack Frost'

Ligustrum sinense 'Variegatum'

Loropetalum, Chinese Witch Hazel, Chinese Fringe
Loropetalum chinense

Origin: Japan, China
Zone(s): 8–10
Drought tolerance: medium

Salt tolerance: low
Type: evergreen
Growth rate: medium

Soil: acidic and well-drained
Exposure: full sun to partial shade
Size: 5' to 6' tall by 6' to 8' wide
Form: broad, spreading, vase-shaped with tiers of arching branches with small green or burgundy foliage
Flower: hanging clusters of fragrant, white or pink flowers with narrow, twisted petals in spring and sporadically through-out summer
Fruit: not applicable
Problems: spider mites, root rot, nematodes, nutrient deficiencies
Uses: shrub border, accent, foundation, massing, tree

Many varieties available, including deep-pink, soft pink, and white with green or burgundy foliage. The Razzleberri Fringe Flower, *Loropetalum chinense rubrum* 'Monraz', is a 6' weeping variety with an equal spread. Coppery foliage matures to an olive green and bears deep-red flowers. 'Burgundy' grows to 6' or more with drooping, arching branches. Flowers are salmon-pink with dark red foliage. 'Hines Purpleleaf' is dense and compact and grows to 6' with hot-pink flowers. New leaves are burgundy and mature to a deep purple. 'Blush' has similar growth but the new leaves are burgundy, maturing to a deep-green with hot-pink flowers. Remove lower branches to train into a small and pretty tree. Needs acidic soil and lots of room to show off its lateral branching habit.

Singapore Holly, Miniature Holly
Malpighia coccigera

Origin: West Indies
Zone(s): 10–11
Drought tolerance: medium

Salt tolerance: medium
Type: evergreen
Growth rate: slow

Soil: rich, moist, and sandy
Exposure: full sun to partial shade
Size: 1' to 3' tall by 2' to 5' wide
Form: dense, rounded with miniature, hollylike green leaves
Flower: 1/2", soft pink, crepelike flowers in spring and summer
Fruit: 1/2", reddish orange berries
Problems: nematodes, scale insects, spider mites
Uses: hedge, accent, massing, shrub border, foundation, container, bird gardens

A pretty and well-behaved shrub. Easy to prune to desired shape and height, making it perfect for formal hedges and borders. Leaves are spiny so use care when handling. *Malpighia punica* 'Dwarf Pink Mound' is compact and easily maintained at 1'. The tree form, *M. glabra* (Barbados Cherry), grows up to 12' tall with an equal canopy spread and bears edible fruit.

Malpighia punica
'Dwarf Pink Mound'

Malpighia punica 'Dwarf Pink Mound'

Turk's Cap, Wax Mallow, Lipstick Hibiscus
Malvaviscus arboreus

Origin: Mexico to Columbia

Zone(s): 9–11

Drought tolerance: high

Salt tolerance: low

Type: evergreen

Growth rate: fast

Soil: tolerant of most

Exposure: full sun

Size: 7' to 12' tall by 8' to 10' wide

Form: upright, spreading with green leaves similar to hibiscus

Flower: red, hibiscus-like buds that never open; flowers year-round

Fruit: not applicable

Problems: none

Uses: hedge, background, accent, screen, bird gardens, specimen

An easy-care plant with constant flowers. Prune to keep scraggly growth in check. Flowers attract birds.

Variegated Tapioca, Variegated Cassava
Manihot esculenta 'Variegata'

Origin: Brazil

Zone(s): 10–12

Drought tolerance: low

Salt tolerance: low

Type: deciduous

Growth rate: fast

Soil: rich, moist, well-drained

Exposure: sun to partial shade

Size: 6' to 8' tall by 4' to 8' wide

Form: upright growth with knobby, pale-yellow stems; leaves consist of numerous large, white leaflets with green tips and bright red stems

Flower: inconspicuous

Fruit: not applicable

Problems: none

Uses: accent, shrub border, container

The variegated tapioca is a member of the cassava family, but this species is grown solely as an ornamental. It has shallow roots and is top-heavy, so avoid planting in windy areas. Although it's spectacular when in leaf, the plant is leafless during the winter. Therefore, it doesn't make a suitable specimen plant. For nontropical locations, dig and store the root over the winter and replant in spring.

Medinilla
Medinilla myriantha

Origin: Philippines
Zone(s): 10–11
Drought tolerance: low
Salt tolerance: low
Type: evergreen
Growth rate: slow

Soil: moist, rich, and acidic
Exposure: filtered light to shade
Size: 3' to 6' tall by 3' to 5' wide
Form: upright with bold, large, soft green leaves
Flower: soft pink, held in pendulous clusters from spring through summer
Fruit: lavender berries
Problems: none
Uses: container, accent, shrub border

An unusual and attractive plant. Does well in containers. Needs moist soil and shade in the afternoon to perform well. A very tender plant suitable for conservatories. *Medinilla magnifica* bears large pink bracts and is suitable for Zones 11 and 12.

Brazilian Red Cloak
Megaskepasma erythrochlamys

Origin: Venezuela

Zone(s): 10–11

Drought tolerance: low

Salt tolerance: low

Type: evergreen

Growth rate: fast

Soil: fertile, moist, and well-drained

Exposure: partial shade to shade

Size: 8' to 12' tall by 6' to 10' wide

Form: upright, broad-spreading, bold form with green, elliptical leaves up to 12" long

Flower: 12" spikes composed of red bracts from which white tubular flowers emerge year-round

Fruit: not applicable

Problems: none

Uses: screen, hedge, background, specimen, bank cover, shrub border

A bold plant with constant flowers. When grown in full sun, foliage becomes yellowish green. Remove spent blooms after their heavy blooming period in spring. Has a broad spread that is controlled by pruning; otherwise, give it space.

Orange Jessamine, Orange Jasmine, Chinese Box
Murraya paniculata

Origin: Southeast Asia   *Salt tolerance:* medium
Zone(s): 9–11   *Type:* evergreen
Drought tolerance: high   *Growth rate:* medium

Soil: tolerant of most well-drained
Exposure: sun to partial shade
Size: 8' to 15' tall by 10' wide
Form: open habit with pendulous branches and glossy, dark
             green leaves divided into 1" leaflets
Flower: white, 3/4", star-shaped, citruslike, fragrant blooms in
             spring and summer
Fruit: red, 1/2" berries
Problems: scale insects, whiteflies, nematodes
Uses: hedge, shrub border, bank cover, specimen, accent, tree,
             screen, background, foundation, container, bird gardens

The Orange Jessamine is a versatile and attractive plant that's a perfect complement to other plants. Remove the lower branches to train into a small, handsome tree. Easy to prune to desired shape and height.

fruit

hedge   flower

Summer Poinsettia
Mussaenda species

Origin: Philippines, Tropical West Africa

Zone(s): 10–11

Drought tolerance: low

Salt tolerance: low

Type: evergreen

Growth rate: fast

Soil:	rich, well-drained, and moist
Exposure:	full sun
Size:	6' to 15' tall
Form:	billowing, soft shape with light green, oval leaves
Flower:	pink, red, or white bracts surround yellow, starlike flowers from spring through autumn
Fruit:	not applicable
Problems:	none
Uses:	container, accent, specimen, foundation, shrub border

Extremely showy genus with many species. Very sensitive to temperatures below 40°F. The Summer Poinsettia, *Mussaenda erythrophylla*, bears pink or red bracts, and *Mussaenda philippica* has white bracts. The Yellow Mussaenda, *Mussaenda incana*, bears a similar star-shaped flower surrounded by yellow bracts. It's twiggy with small, green leaves and grows to 6' by 4'. The incana variety is more cold tolerant than its flamboyant relatives.

Mussaenda erythrophylla
'Dona Luz'

Mussaenda incana

Mussaenda philippica
'Dona Aurora'

Oleander
Nerium oleander

Origin: Eurasia

Zone(s): 8–11

Drought tolerance: high

Salt tolerance: high

Type: evergreen

Growth rate: medium

Soil:	tolerant of most with good drainage
Exposure:	full sun to partial shade
Size:	10' to 18' tall by 6' to12' wide
Form:	upright, round with long bamboolike, dull green foliage
Flower:	fragrant, single or double flowers in white, pink, or red from spring through autumn
Fruit:	long, thin seedpods
Problems:	oleander caterpillar, leaf scorch (bacterial disease), nematodes, scale insects
Uses:	hedge, background, screen, accent, shrub border

Free flowering with willowy stems. Dwarf varieties, 'Petite Salmon' and 'Petite Pink', grow to 4' with an equal spread. In Florida, the oleander caterpillar is a serious problem. In California, Arizona, and Texas, leaf scorch, which is spread by the sharpshooter insect, is a major concern. Oleander is suitable for containers and foundation plantings. It is poisonous if ingested. Do not compost trimmings and don't burn the wood, as fumes are also toxic.

Nerium oleander

Nerium oleander (single pink)

Nerium oleander (double pink)

Nerium oleander 'Petite Salmon'

Firespike, Cardinal Spear
Odontonema strictum

Origin: Central America
Zone(s): 9–11
Drought tolerance: medium

Salt tolerance: low
Type: evergreen
Growth rate: fast

Soil: tolerant of most
Exposure: partial shade
Size: 3' to 6' tall by 2' to 3' wide
Form: bold, bushy with large, elliptical, green leaves
Flower: crimson, tubular flowers on 4"-to-12"-long spikes year-round
Fruit: not applicable
Problems: none
Uses: hedge, screen, background, foundation, accent, specimen, massing, shrub border

Very showy flowers similar to red salvia. Attracts butterflies and birds, including hummingbirds. Firespike seeds readily and may become invasive.

Golden Shrimp Plant
Pachystachys lutea

Origin: Peru   *Salt tolerance:* low
Zone(s): 9–11   *Type:* evergreen
Drought tolerance: low   *Growth rate:* fast
Soil: moist, well-drained, and fertile
Exposure: partial shade to sun
Size: 2' to 3' tall and wide
Form: upright, bushy with elliptical, green leaves
Flower: upright spikes composed of yellow bracts surrounding white,
          tubular flowers year-round
Fruit: not applicable
Problems: scale insects
Uses: accent, specimen, container, foundation, bird gardens,
                 shrub border

A beautiful and carefree plant that blooms freely. Best where it receives morning sun and afternoon shade. Flowers attract humming-birds.

Pittosporum, Pitts.
Pittosporum tobira

Origin: Japan, China
Zone(s): 8–11
Drought tolerance: medium
Salt tolerance: high

Type: evergreen
Growth rate: fast when young
but slows with age

Soil:	tolerant of most with good drainage
Exposure:	sun to partial shade
Size:	8' to 12' tall and wide
Form:	dense, rounded shape with whorls of narrow, oval leaves
Flower:	fragrant, small, creamy white in spring
Fruit:	not applicable
Problems:	scale insects, leafspots, aphids, nematodes, leaf spot, root rot, mealybugs, sooty mold
Uses:	foundation, hedge, mass planting, container, shrub border, bank cover, small tree, lanai

Scale insects, aphids, and sooty mold are notable problems in south Florida. 'Wheeler's Dwarf' is 3' by 5' and is susceptible to root rot. 'Variegata' bears green foliage edged in cream. Micronutrient deficiencies are common in alkaline soils. Mature plants age into attractive trees.

Pittosporum tobira

Pittosporum tobira 'Variegata'

Plumbago, Leadwort
Plumbago auriculata

Origin: South Africa
Zone(s): 10–11
Drought tolerance: high once
         established

Salt tolerance: medium
Type: evergreen
Growth rate: medium

Soil:	tolerant of most soils
Exposure:	partial shade to full sun
Size:	5' to 7' tall and wide
Form:	loose, sprawling with arching branches and small, green leaves
Flower:	phloxlike in shades of blue or white, depending on variety; held in 6" clusters most of the year
Fruit:	small, cylindrical seed heads
Problems:	scale insects, spider mites, nematodes
Uses:	hedge, shrub border, massing, bank cover, butterfly gardens, foundation, containers

New species have deep-blue flowers, which are an improvement on the standard pale blue color. These include 'Royal Cape', 'Imperial Blue', and 'Escapade Blue'. 'Escapade White', 'Alba', and 'White Cape' are white varieties. Plumbagos are easy plants that benefit from regular shearing to promote flowering and keep them compact. Plants send out underground runners close to the mother plant when they mature, so they are slightly invasive. Blossoms provide nectar for butterflies and food for their larvae.

Podocarpus, Japanese Yew Pine
Podocarpus macrophyllus

Origin: Japan

Zone(s): 7–11

Drought tolerance: medium

Salt tolerance: medium

Type: evergreen

Growth rate: medium

Soil: tolerant of most soils

Exposure: full sun to partial shade

Size: 35' to 50' tall

Form: tree or shrub; dense, upright, bushy with flat, needlelike, 4" foliage

Flower: inconspicuous beige catkins in early summer

Fruit: bluish purple berries

Problems: aphids, scale insects, sooty mold

Uses: houseplant, topiary, bird gardens, tree, hedge, shrub border, screen, foundation, background

Versatile tree that is often grown as a shrub or large hedge. When grown as a tree, it generally grows to 50' with a 25' canopy, but it's easily maintained at 6' to 8' by 4' to 6' as a compact shrub. Grows full and lush even at its base. Tends to grow looser and slower in shade. There are numerous Podocarpus species available, but the macrophyllus is best suited to grow as a shrub.

Aralia
Polyscias species

Origin: South Pacific   *Salt tolerance:* medium
Zone(s): 10–11   *Type:* evergreen
Drought tolerance: high   *Growth rate:* medium

Soil: tolerant of most but prefers rich, moist, well-drained
Exposure: full sun to shade
Size: 6' to 10' tall by 2' to 5' wide, depending on species
Form: upright, generally narrow
Flower: inconspicuous
Fruit: not applicable
Problems: aphids, thrips, mites
Uses: container, bonsai, foundation, accent, hedge, tree, house-
              plant, specimen, shrub border, lanai, bird and Asian gar-
              dens

Their shape and texture deliver an Oriental feel. To emphasize their
Asian look, remove the lower leaves. Chicken Gizzard Aralia
(Geranium leaf), *Polyscias crispata*, grows to 7' and bears round, lobed
foliage on bushy plants. The Ming Aralia, *Polyscias fruticosa* 'Elegans',
has parsleylike foliage on 6' by 4' plants. The Fernleaf Aralia, *Polyscias
filicifolia*, has finely cut, feathery foliage on 8' by 5' plants. Variegated
evergreen Aralia, *Polyscias pinnata* 'Marginata', has foliage edged in
white and grows to 20' by 8'. The Dinner Plate Aralia (Balfour
Aralia), *Polyscias* pinnata, grows to 6' by 4' and has large, round
leaves. The Oakleaf Aralia, *Polyscias obtusa*, grows to a narrow 6'. The
Rose-leaf Aralia, *Polyscias guilfoylei*, bears pendant, serrated leaves, similar to large rose leaves, on tall, 10', willowy stems.

Polyscias crispata

Polyscias pinnata 'Marginata'

Polyscias guilfoylei 'Marginata'

Shooting Star Shrub, Amethyst Star
Pseuderanthemum laxiflorum

Origin: Polynesia   *Salt tolerance:* medium
Zone(s): 10–11   *Type:* evergreen
Drought tolerance: low   *Growth rate:* fast
Soil: prefers rich, moist, well-drained
Exposure: partial shade to sun
Size: 3' to 4' tall by 3' wide
Form: upright, twiggy with shiny, green, oval leaves
Flower: 3/4", starlike, deep-purple flowers year-round
Fruit: not applicable
Problems: scale insects
Uses: accent, container, foundation, shrub border

A well-behaved and easy shrub that doesn't get too tall or too wide.
Prune to keep compact.

Wild Coffee
Psychotria nervosa

Origin: south Florida, West Indies
Zone(s): 10–11
Drought tolerance: medium

Salt tolerance: medium
Type: evergreen
Growth rate: fast

Soil:	tolerant of most
Exposure:	partial shade to shade
Size:	4' to 10' tall by 4' to 8' wide
Form:	upright with dark green, slightly puckered, glossy, oval leaves and deeply cut veins
Flower:	tiny, white, starlike flowers in spring and summer
Fruit:	clusters of small red berries
Problems:	scale insects occasionally
Uses:	background, shrub border, massing, hedge, foundation, accent, container, bird gardens

An attractive, easy-care plant due to its lateral branching pattern and rich, green foliage. Easy to prune to desired height. The fruit attracts birds.

Psychotria nervosa with fruit

Psychotria nervosa flowers

Psychotria nervosa berries

Indian Hawthorn
Rhaphiolepis indica

Origin: China   *Salt tolerance:* medium
Zone(s): 8–11   *Type:* evergreen
Drought tolerance: high   *Growth rate:* slow

Soil: tolerant of most soils but prefers fertile, well-drained soils
Exposure: sun to partial shade
Size: 2' to 4' tall and wide
Form: compact, round, dense growth with dull, leathery, gray-green leaves up to 3" long
Flower: clusters of fragrant, 3/4", white or pink flowers in spring and occasionally in fall
Fruit: small purple-black berries
Problems: fireblight, scale insects, nematodes, leafspot
Uses: foundation, shrub border, massing, container

A tough, resilient plant that's also beautiful. Seldom needs pruning due to its compact form and slow growth rate. Does best in partial shade. 'Ballerina' grows to 1' to 2' with dark pink flowers. 'Enchantress Pink' is a dwarf with a show from late winter to early spring. 'Fascination' has dense, compact growth with pink, star-shaped flowers with white centers. 'Jack Evans' is dense with double pink blossoms. 'Springtime' has bronze leaves with pink flowers and is a faster grower than its relatives.

Rhaphiolepis indica

Rhaphiolepis indica fruit

Azalea
Rhododendron

Origin: China, Japan
Zone(s): 7–10
Drought tolerance: low

Salt tolerance: low
Type: evergreen
Growth rate: medium

Soil: rich, acidic, moist, well-drained soils
Exposure: shade
Size: depends on species and variety
Form: dense, spreading with oval, dull green leaves
Flower: clusters of 1"-to-3", single or double flared blossoms in red, pink, orange, and lavender
Fruit: not applicable
Problems: nutrient deficiencies, root rot, scale insects, leafspot
Uses: foundation, container, accent, massing

Although many tropical gardeners shy away from azaleas, thinking they are only for more temperate climes, there are a few plants that do nicely in tropical climates when given the proper care. The Southern Indian Azalea, *Rhododendron indica*, is a relatively tall species growing from 5' to 10' and may be pruned into small trees by removing the lower limbs. It has large, 2"-to-4" single flowers. Kurume, or Dwarf, Azaleas, *Rhododendron kurume*, grow from 2' to 6' with 1"-to-2" single or double blossoms. Azaleas prefer sun in the morning for only a few hours followed by shade in the afternoon. The soil must be acidic with a pH of 4.5 to 5.5. Use at least a 3" layer of organic mulch. Avoid planting against a building foundation as the alkaline properties of the concrete leach into the surrounding soil. Keep the soil moist, especially until the plants become established. Azaleas dislike being pruned and require only an errant branch to be cut back occasionally. Prune, if necessary, directly after flowering.

Rhododendron indica

Rhododendron kurume

Vireya Rhododendron
Rhododendron vireya

Origin: Southeast Asia   *Salt tolerance:* low
Zone(s): 10–11   *Type:* evergreen
Drought tolerance: low   *Growth rate:* slow
Soil: rich, moist, acidic, well-drained soils
Exposure: shade
Size: up to 4', depending on variety
Form: depends on variety
Flower: clusters of flared trumpets sporadically throughout the year
Fruit: not applicable
Problems: nutrient deficiencies, scale insects, mealybugs
Uses: specimen, accent, shrub border, foundation, container

Vireyas are uncommon but are becoming more popular for their beauty and frequent flowering. A stunning shrub for tropical locations as well as a novelty container plant in cooler climates. There are many types, shapes, and sizes of vireyas, from ground covers to shrubs. Some have large 3" dramatic blossoms, while others have petite, modest flowers. Many are fragrant. Colors include white, red, pink, and combinations thereof. They prefer sun in the morning and shade during the afternoon. Like azaleas, they need an acidic, rich, moist soil. Mulch with 3" of organic mulch and keep soil moist until vireyas become established.

Rhododendron vireya
'George Bungen'

Rose
Rosa species and hybrids

Origin: Europe, Asia, North America
Zone(s): 4–11
Drought tolerance: medium

Salt tolerance: low
Type: deciduous; evergreen in Zones 10 and 11
Growth rate: fast

Soil: rich, slightly acidic soils
Exposure: full sun
Size: 6" to 8' tall
Form: depends on species and variety
Flower: depends on species and variety
Fruit: rose hips on some species are yellow, red, or orange
Problems: aphids, spider mites, nematodes, thrips, rose beetle, powdery mildew, blackspot
Uses: cut flower, container, foundation, shrub border, hedge, accent, specimen

China, teas, and other old garden roses are the easiest to grow in the tropics. 'Old Blush' and 'Louis Philippe' are both China roses and grow to 8'. Both are relatively thornless, bear clusters of 1"-to-2", double, fragrant flowers. 'Old Blush' has pink flowers, while 'Louis Phillipe' has red. 'Mrs. B. R. Cant' is a tea rose (not to be confused with hybrid teas), grows to 5', and bears deep-pink clusters of 1"-to-2" fragrant blossoms most of the year. Although the teas and Chinas are tall, they are easy to prune and are the most resistant of all roses to aphids, mildew, and blackspot. 'Red Cascade' is a tough, hardy miniature with small, red, unscented roses most of the year. It grows to 6" in height and has long, sprawling canes that can be trained to climb. Suitable hybrid tea roses must be grafted onto the Fortuniana rootstock. Hybrid teas are more difficult to grow than old-fashioned roses; however, some are better than others for the tropics. 'Tropicana' grows to 8' with 4", soft orange, fragrant, double blossoms most of the year. 'Mr. Lincoln' has double, deep-red, velvet, fragrant flowers on 5', thorny plants. 'Don Juan' is an excellent climbing hybrid tea. It bears large, deep-red, velvet 4" flowers held in large clusters all year and grows to 10'. Check with local sources for the roses that do well in your area.

'Tropicana'

'Old Blush'

'Louis Philippe'

'Mrs. B.R. Cant'

'Don Juan'

'Red Cascade'

Firecracker Plant
Russelia equisetiformis

Origin: Mexico, Central America
Zone(s): 9–11
Drought tolerance: high

Salt tolerance: high
Type: evergreen
Growth rate: medium

Soil: tolerant of most soils
Exposure: full sun
Size: 3' to 4' tall by 6' to 12' wide
Form: a weeping, fountain shape with rushlike stems with a few small, narrow leaves
Flower: red, tubular, and borne along willowy stems year-round
Fruit: small, pendant clusters
Problems: nematodes
Uses: accent, foundation, container, massing, specimen, bank cover, hedge, shrub border

The profuse, colorful flowers, wispy texture, and cascading fountain shape are eye catching. A chartreuse variety is also available. Spreads by underground runners; branches tend to root when they touch the ground. It's considered slightly invasive, so give it plenty of room.

Rutty
Ruttyruspolia 'Phyllis Van Heeden'

Origin: Africa

Zone(s): 10–11

Drought tolerance: medium

Salt tolerance: low

Type: evergreen

Growth rate: medium

Soil: rich, well-drained soils

Exposure: full sun

Size: 3' to 4' tall and wide

Form: fountainlike, arching branches and green, oval leaves

Flower: 3" dense clusters of purple-pink flowers year-round

Fruit: not applicable

Problems: none

Uses: hedge, accent, shrub border, foundation

An uncommon but beautiful shrub. Arching branches produce many flower spikes along the stems and at branch tips. Stems sometimes root along the ground, producing new plants. Prune yearly to keep compact.

Sanchezia
Sanchezia speciosa

Origin: Ecuador
Zone(s): 10–11
Drought tolerance: low

Salt tolerance: medium
Type: evergreen
Growth rate: fast

Soil: tolerant of most soils but prefers moist soils
Exposure: sun to partial shade
Size: 8' tall and wide
Form: bold and wide with large, green, oval leaves with yellow veins
Flower: spikes of reddish orange bracts containing yellow, tubular flowers in spring, summer, and autumn
Fruit: not applicable
Problems: mealybugs, spider mites, nematodes
Uses: shrub border, screen, hedge

An unusual plant with foliage as flashy as its flowers. Give it room to spread.

Aralia Schefflera, Dwarf Schefflera, Arboricola
Schefflera arboricola

Origin: Taiwan

Zone(s): 10–11

Drought tolerance: high

Salt tolerance: medium

Type: evergreen

Growth rate: medium

Soil: tolerant of most soils

Exposure: full sun to shade

Size: 6' to 10' tall and wide

Form: rounded, bold shape with 7 to 9 shiny, leathery, green, 3" leaflets comprising one leaf

Flower: insignificant

Fruit: not applicable

Problems: scale insects, mealybugs

Uses: houseplant, container, hedge, massing, lanai, accent, foundation, shrub border

Easy to prune to any size and usually maintained from 2' to 4'. Numerous varieties bear attractive yellow and green variegated foliage. An easy plant that always looks good. Aerial roots from the lower portions of the branches root into the ground, providing firm support and a wide girth.

Schefflera arboricola

Schefflera arboricola 'Trinette'

False Aralia
Schefflera (Dizygotheca) elegantissima

Origin: New Caledonia
Zone(s): 10–11
Drought tolerance: medium

Salt tolerance: medium
Type: evergreen
Growth rate: medium

Soil: rich, moist soils

Exposure: full sun to partial shade

Size: 6' to 25' tall with 6' to 15' canopy

Form: multiple trunks and narrow, upright form with thin, green leaflets originating from a central point

Flower: chartreuse flower clusters up to 1' long in spring

Fruit: inconspicuous, fleshy, and brown in large clusters when mature

Problems: scale insects

Uses: accent, shrub border, container, houseplant, specimen, tree, foundation

Juvenile foliage is small, lacey, glossy, and fine and becomes bolder, with jagged edges and a dull green color, when mature. Its texture and shape has an Oriental feel so it's perfect for a Japanese garden. Grows straight up with most of the foliage on the upper half with bare stems below.

Candle Bush
Senna (Cassia) alata

Origin: Tropical America
Zone(s): 10–11
Drought tolerance: medium

Salt tolerance: medium
Type: evergreen
Growth rate: fast

Soil: tolerant of most soils
Exposure: full sun
Size: 8' to 10' tall by 4' to 8' wide
Form: bushy shrub with deep-green leaves
Flower: erect yellow flowers that resemble candles from spring through fall
Fruit: long, brown seedpods
Problems: caterpillars
Uses: accent, butterfly gardens, shrub border

A striking and attractive plant. Cut back often and especially after flowering to keep compact. Seedlings may be a problem. Cassias are larval food and provide nectar for sulfur butterflies.

Cassia
Senna (Cassia) bicapsularis

Origin: Caribbean   *Salt tolerance:* medium
Zone(s): 10–11   *Type:* evergreen
Drought tolerance: medium   *Growth rate:* fast
Soil: tolerant of most soils
Exposure: full sun
Size: 10' to 12' tall by 10' wide
Form: shrubby, robust, wide, spreading, vinelike
Flower: 2" yellow flowers in clusters from spring through fall
Fruit: long, brown pods
Problems: caterpillars, twig borers
Uses: butterfly gardens, accent, shrub border

Very pretty, airy plant. Cassias are larval food and provide nectar for sulfur butterflies. Prune to desired shape and height. Stake to keep upright. Considered invasive.

Bird of Paradise, Orange Bird of Paradise, Crane Flower
Strelitzia reginae

Origin: South Africa
Zone(s): 9–11
Drought tolerance: high
Salt tolerance: low

Type: evergreen non-woody perennial
Growth rate: medium

Soil:	rich, moist, and well-drained
Exposure:	full sun
Size:	3' to 4' tall and wide
Form:	upright, vase-shaped with stiff, paddle-shaped leaves
Flower:	odd-looking with 3 orange petals and 3 blue held horizontally and singly on leafless stems in summer and autumn
Fruit:	not applicable
Problems:	scale insects, mealybugs
Uses:	foundation, specimen, accent, massing, containers, lanai

A striking, bold architectural perennial that is technically not a shrub since it's non-woody. The tough, gray-green leaves are wind resistant. Needs full sun and high-phosphorus or high-potash fertilizers with low nitrogen to flower well. *Strelitzia juncea* bears reedlike stems and smaller flowers. The Cape Wild Banana, *Strelitzia alba*, bears white flowers on 6'-to-10' plants. The White Bird of Paradise, *Strelitzia nicolai*, is a huge relative, reaching 30' by 30', with large white flowers.

Strelitzia reginae
flower

Strelitzia reginae

Strelitzia nicolai
flower

Strelitzia nicolai

Crepe Jasmine, Cape Jasmine, Butterfly Gardenia, Pinwheel Jasmine
Tabernaemontana divaricata

Origin: India

Zone(s): 10–11

Drought tolerance: low

Salt tolerance: medium

Type: evergreen

Growth rate: medium

Soil: prefers acidic, rich soil

Exposure: full sun to partial shade

Size: 6' to10' tall by 4' to 8' wide

Form: lateral branching, broad habit with deep-green, glossy, oval leaves

Flower: slightly scented, crepelike, pure white flowers appear sporadically throughout the year

Fruit: not applicable

Problems: scale insects, mites, sooty mold, nematodes

Uses: foundation, small tree, accent, specimen, background, screen, shrub border, hedge

Very beautiful flowers with rich foliage and an attractive lateral branching pattern. Does best when shaded from the afternoon sun. Single and double forms available. 'Flore Pleno' (Crepe Jasmine, Butterfly Gardenia) bears slightly scented, 2", double blossoms. 'Pinwheel Jasmine' has 1", single, white flowers with a small, yellow eye in the center and grows to 5' by 5'.

Tabernaemontana divaricata

Tabernaemontana divaricata 'Flore Pleno'

Tabernaemontana divaricata 'Pinwheel'

Tabernaemontana divaricata 'Pinwheel'

Yellow Elder, Yellow Trumpet Flower
Tecoma stans

Origin: Caribbean
Zone(s): 10–11
Drought tolerance: high
Salt tolerance: medium

Type: evergreen shrub or small tree
Growth rate: fast

Soil:	tolerant to most soils
Exposure:	full sun
Size:	15' to 30' tall
Form:	upright form that droops with age; has oval, irregular crown with bright-green, serrated leaves
Flower:	bright-yellow, fragrant, tubular flowers borne in clusters primarily in the autumn
Fruit:	thin, long, hard, brown pods
Problems:	none
Uses:	specimen, accent, small tree, shrub border, container

A beautiful plant that grows to a 15' shrub or a 30' tree. Although its primary flowering time is autumn, it sends out a few blossoms each time it flushes out with more leaves. A great plant that always looks good.

Cape Honeysuckle
Tecomaria capensis

Origin: India
Zone(s): 10–11
Drought tolerance: medium

Salt tolerance: medium
Type: evergreen
Growth rate: fast

Soil: tolerant of most soils
Exposure: full sun
Size: 4' to 8' tall by 5' to 8' wide as a shrub, 20' as a vine
Form: sprawling shrub or vine with green, fernlike foliage
Flower: bright orange-red, 2", flaring, tubular flowers in elongat-ed clusters during summer and autumn
Fruit: long, narrow, flatted capsules
Problems: scale insects, spider mites, nematodes
Uses: hedge, screen, bank cover, shrub border

A rampant grower that easily takes over its allotted space. however, it adapts well to pruning and shearing. Often used as a shrub rather than a vine. *Tecomaria capensis* 'Aurea' bears yellow flowers.

Bush Clock Vine, King's Mantle
Thunbergia erecta

Origin: Africa		*Salt tolerance:* medium	
Zone(s): 10–11		*Type:* evergreen	
Drought tolerance: medium		*Growth rate:* fast	

Soil: tolerant of most soils

Exposure: full sun to partial shade

Size: 3' to 5' tall by 4' to 6' wide

Form: upright with small, dark green leaves on thin stems

Flower: deep-purple, upturned, 2", flared tubular flowers with a yellow throat year-round

Fruit: inconspicuous

Problems: none

Uses: hedge, container, shrub border, background, accent, screen, foundation

An easy and attractive shrub. Leaves are small so it's easy to prune and shear to any size and shape. Prune to keep plant compact. 'Alba' is a white flowering form. The King's Mantle is an exception to the Thunbergia genus, as its many relatives are vines.

Princess Flower, Glorybush
Tibouchina urvilleana

Origin: Brazil   *Salt tolerance:* low
Zone(s): 9–11   *Type:* evergreen
Drought tolerance: low   *Growth rate:* medium
Soil: rich, acidic soils with good drainage
Exposure: partial shade
Size: 10' tall and wide
Form: upright, loose with velvetlike, soft green leaves up to 6"
             long
Flower: deep-purple, flat, 3" flowers most of the year
Fruit: not applicable
Problems: spider mites, root rot, nematodes
Uses: specimen, accent, foundation, shrub border, informal
             hedge

Its flowers add a bold purple accent to the garden, while its foliage provides a soft touch. Prune back when it becomes leggy or grows too large. Does best in an eastern exposure. Difficult to establish so keep soil moist until new growth appears, and avoid hot, sunny sites. Has naturalized in Hawaii.

Sandankwa Viburnum; Sweet Viburnum
Viburnum suspensum; Viburnum odoratissimum

Origin: Asia

Zone(s): 8–10

Drought tolerance: medium

Salt tolerance: low

Type: evergreen

Growth rate: medium

Soil: tolerant of most soils but prefers rich loam

Exposure: sun to partial shade

Size: depends on species

Form: depends on species

Flower: small, white clusters of fragrant flowers in spring

Fruit: small, red berries that turn black

Problems: scale insects, nematodes

Uses: hedge, screen, barrier, background, shrub border, massing, foundation, bird and butterfly gardens

Viburnums suitable for tropical climates generally don't have the beautiful flower sprays of their northern cousins, but they're valued for other qualities. Their ability to attract birds and butterflies to the garden, combined with their attractive foliage, dense habit, fragrance, versatility, and hardiness, make them winners. Viburnum flowers are larval food for butterflies, and birds love their black berries. The Sandankwa Viburnum, *Viburnum suspensum,* grows to 6' by 6', with 4", coarse, deep-green leaves and bears clusters of small, pinkish white flowers with little fragrance. Sweet Viburnum, *Viburnum odoratissimum,* grows to 15' but it is easily maintained at 8'. It bears clusters of small but fragrant flowers. The Awabuki, or Mirror-leafed, Viburnum, *Viburnum odoratissimum* 'Awabuki', is a vigorous plant growing to 12' to 20' with shiny, 8", deep-green leaves. It bears 3"-to-6" clusters of white, fragrant flowers.

Viburnum suspensum hedge

Viburnum suspensum flowers

Variegated Vitex
Vitex trifolia 'Variegata'

Origin: Asia, Australia *Salt tolerance:* medium
Zone(s): 9–11 *Type:* evergreen
Drought tolerance: medium *Growth rate:* medium

Soil: tolerant of most soils but prefers well-drained, moist soils
Exposure: full sun
Size: 10' to 20' tall by 8' to 12' wide
Form: upright and dense with green and white variegated leaves
Flower: clusters of 1/2" lavender flowers in summer
Fruit: clusters of small brown berries
Problems: mushroom root rot, scale insects
Uses: hedge, shrub border, accent, screen, tree, foundation, butterfly gardens

The undersides of the foliage are soft like velvet and the topsides are green edged in white. An added bonus is its light mauve flowers that attract butterflies. Leaves smell when crushed. Grow as a small tree by removing the lower limbs. Keep moist until established. Prune to keep bushy after flowering.

Vitex trifolia 'Variegata'

Vitex trifolia 'Variegata' hedge

THE HEALTHY
TROPICAL GARDEN

THE RIGHT PLANT IN THE RIGHT PLACE

Once a landscape has been installed, it is heartbreaking to see hundreds of dollars worth of plants die because they were planted in the wrong place. Whether you're designing a new landscape, rearranging an existing one, or just adding a new shrub, it's essential to keep a few things in mind before sliding the shovel into the ground.

To ensure success it's important to duplicate a plant's native habitat. People who have green thumbs don't plant shade-loving specimens in full sun. They avoid planting bog plants in raised beds or acid-loving plants in beach sand. They consider correct drainage, salt tolerance, soil fertility, pH, sun exposure, and planting procedures whenever they plant something in the ground. When you give plants what they like, they respond favorably.

EXPOSURE

As the sun rises in the east, it provides the perfect light for plants preferring partial shade. The morning sun dries the dew and plants wake gently with nature's soft hand. The light intensifies as the sun heads south, withering weak, shade-loving, and temperate flora with its unrelenting tropical zeal.

Although western exposures are in shadows during the morning hours, by the afternoon the temperature and light intensify, making it an ideal location for heat-tolerant shrubs. Cool northern exposures are also cloaked in morning shade, but during the summer the sun lingers in the sky and offers light to otherwise shadowed nooks.

Before you plant, it's important to know where the sunny and shady parts are in your yard. Numerous problems occur when planting sun worshippers in a shady nook. As their vigor declines, insects and diseases take hold. Some variegated plants may lose their vivid colors, and flowering plants will cease to blossom. Alternately, shade-loving shrubs will wilt, become pale, and grow leggy when situated in inhospitable, sunny areas.

MICROCLIMATES

Every garden has at least one microclimate, where the environmental conditions differ from those in the rest of the yard. These microclimates are hotter, cooler, or windier than the surrounding area. Structures and trees produce shade and temper the sun. Reflective surfaces such as cement increase light and heat, while wind desiccates and batters plants.

Microclimates can be a good thing or a bad thing, depending on their type. Luckily, most situations can be modified with a little creativity and know-how.

Remember that houses, fences, walls, sheds, and large plants produce shade. The depth of the shade produced is seasonal. Shadows are longer in winter because the sun is low, and shorter in summer because the sun hangs high in the sky. There are also more daylight hours in the summer than in winter.

A hot area in the garden may be

Partial shade is created by the many limbs from the overhead trees.

The white stones and a lack of living, green material turn this garden into a hot microclimate.

112

caused by reflected light from the white walls of a house or from surrounding concrete, such as a paved walkway or driveway. Pale or white rock mulch also intensifies light and increases the temperature in full sun. Alternately, black and dark-colored items, including organic mulch, absorb light so the surroundings are softer and cooler.

You can mollify extreme conditions by using a little paint and imagination. In shady areas, remove overhead tree limbs or paint the surrounding structures white to reflect light. Use mirrors to illuminate dark areas. To darken and cool a location that is too bright, paint any surrounding structures a dark color or place deep-green shrubs against them. Arbors and screens positioned on the south side of a garden instantly provide shade and add a dramatic vertical element to the landscape.

Too much or too little sun isn't the only natural element gardeners have to deal with. Gusty gales on the windward sides of islands, coastlines, and peninsulas suck moisture out of plant tissues, parch soils, distort growth, and bring not only wet weather but savage storms. Windbreaks alleviate Mother Nature's attacks naturally and effectively by providing a buffer. Where damage due to salt spray is a problem, select salt-tolerant plants with thick, dense, evergreen growth to block the wind. Plant two or three rows instead of a single row for an attractive and effective barrier.

SIZE

There is nothing more annoying than a plant that exceeds your expectations to the extent that it overtakes its allotted spot and becomes a nuisance. Most shrubs are originally container grown so their roots are confined, restricting their growth. Once planted in the ground, they breathe a sigh of relief as their roots and stems grow as nature intended.

Most shrubs found in nurseries are in their baby stage. They look cute, perfect, neat, and compact, and beg you to take them home. Many of these babies develop into giants. Take oleander, for example. Most people don't realize this common tropical shrub can grow to 16 feet in height.

Although plant height is an important consideration, so is width. Very few plants are narrow, especially in the tropics. Many are full and lush and oftentimes grow as wide as they are tall. Not only can oleander reach the ultimate height of 16 feet, it can also expand to a width of 12 feet. Of course, this is under ideal conditions.

Shrubs that grow too big for their allotted space are a maintenance nightmare. Most tropical plants are not timid little creatures. They grow with gay abandon and it's difficult to keep them in check. Instead of falling into this trap, look for other selections that will fill the bill and be a pleasure rather than a nuisance.

Although many plant reference materials usually give a plant's height and sometimes its width, this information is not written in stone. It is difficult to determine the ultimate size of shrubs because their environment, maintenance, and genetics play key roles in their growth. Soil and weather vary considerably in the tropi-

Although most bougainvilleas don't become this enormous, this one has never seen pruners. Its flowers are pretty, but this tree dominates even a big yard.

cal sections of the United States. A shrub grown in Hawaii will respond and grow differently than the same one grown in Florida, California, or Arizona. In fact, two identical shrubs planted in the same garden may react differently because the soil, light, wind, and moisture aren't exactly the same from one end of the garden to the other. Fertilizing, watering, pruning, and other forms of maintenance also determine a plant's size. If a shrub receives what it needs when it needs it, it will grow to its full potential. On the other hand, if it is neglected, it will fall short of its estimated height and width. And since many plants are not clones (not yet anyway), genetics also determine their growth habits.

The mature size for each shrub is included with its entry in the Shrub Encyclopedia. The appendix includes two separate lists, one denoting the mature height of each shrub and the other, the maintainable height. Mature height refers to a shrub's non-pruned proportions while maintainable height refers to a shrub's typical size when pruned annually. Since most gardeners prune their plants a couple of times a year, a shrub's mature height can be deceiving. Although some shrubs grow to gigantic proportions, they are generally restrained to more suitable dimensions with a pair of pruners.

VARIETIES

Taxonomy, the science of classifying plants, groups plants together with similar genetic characteristics. A plant's genus denotes which branch of the plant kingdom it belongs to. For example, the white chenille plant's botanical name is *Acalypha hispida* 'Alba'. The first name, *Acalypha,* is the genus. The second name, *hispida,* is the species. The species breaks down the genus by grouping closely related plants together that are able to interbreed because they are genetically similar. The variety, 'Alba', is a variation of the species created from hybridization. Not all plants have varieties. The common red chenille plant, *Acalypha hispida,* is the true species and not a variety, as evidenced by the lack of a third name.

Years ago, plant selection was relatively easy because there were few varieties. Variations are now the norm because of hybridization. Plants that once had only a few relatives now have countless second and third cousins.

This is the normal-size oleander.

This oleander is a dwarf.

There are so many different varieties, it's sometimes difficult to distinguish which genus a plant belongs to. If you've formed a prejudice after a bad experience with a plant, it's still possible a half-sister or a cousin would be perfect. If you think an oleander is too big for your landscape, think again. The Petite Pink and Petite Salmon varieties grow to only 4 feet high, unlike their 16-foot-tall cousins.

Of course, oleander is not the only plant that boasts relatives that break the rules. Most genera, especially non-natives, are bred to provide gardeners with a breathtaking assortment of varieties. Many are mentioned in this text, but it is difficult to include all of them. Some genera simply have too many varieties, and new varieties pop up every year.

SOIL TYPE

Soils vary from one end of the garden to the other, never mind from state to state. It is critical to know what type of soil you have before you waste time, money, and your back on soil amendments that may cause more harm than good.

It is a typical practice to lime gardens in the spring, but many tropical soils are alkaline. Adding lime increases the soil's alkalinity, making it inhospitable for most plants, which prefer slightly acidic conditions. A soil test is a valuable tool, especially if you're new to an area and your plants are not growing well. Healthy soil makes gardening a pleasure, but poor soil turns a wonderful hobby into drudgery.

One of the critical factors for healthy soil is its hydrogen ion concentration (pH), which refers to a soil's alkalinity or acidity. It is rated on a scale from 0 to 14, with 7 being neutral. Below seven is acidic and above is alkaline (also referred to as sweet soil). Most plants prefer a slightly acidic soil at 6.0 to 6.8.

A common sign of alkaline soil is a lack of weeds. Most people are pleased to have few or no weeds, but unless you have been actively working to remove them, you've got trouble. On the other hand, a lot of weeds means your soil is good. So the next time you're cursing them, be thankful they're thriving.

The tropical zones of California, Florida, and Arizona tend to have alkaline soils with a pH of 8.0 or above. This causes many problems, especially when you're growing non-native ornamentals that require acidic conditions. The nutrients become locked in the soil, even after fertilizing, and the plants are unable to absorb the nutrients. You'll often find deficiencies in iron, manganese, and magnesium. Plants become yellow, lack vigor, and succumb to pests and diseases as they slowly starve to death. Sulfur and other acidifying products are useful for short-term use, but the best way to decrease the pH is to add organic matter and use an organic mulch, such as pine needles or whatever is recommended and available locally. Organic matter prevents the soil from deteriorating as it binds the coarse sand particles together. It also provides essential food for the beneficial

Azaleas and other acid-loving plants starve and turn yellow when their soil pH is too high.

microorganisms that inhabit the soil. Since an organic-rich soil retains more nutrients and moisture, watering and fertilizing are reduced.

Although there are isolated pockets of sweet soil, most of the Hawaiian Islands have soils that are too acidic, which brings a new set of problems to the table. Calcium, phosphorus, and magnesium become unavailable for plants to absorb. Calcium deficiencies are a real dilemma. Young leaves are unable to unfurl fully and their tips turn brown and die. Phosphorus deficiencies are denoted by purple foliage. A green V shape surrounded by yellow at the base of leaves is a symptom of magnesium deficiency. Aluminum and manganese toxicity are also associated with acidic soils. Too much aluminum promotes stubby, shortened, and swollen roots. Excess manganese results in stunted, crinkled, and yellow leaves, especially at the top portion of a plant.

The way to correct acidic soils is to add lime. There are many liming products on the market. One of the best is dolomite lime. Hydrated lime tends to burn when not used correctly. Dolomite lime is less likely to burn and it contains magnesium as well as calcium, which is a great bonus where calcium- and magnesium-poor soils prevail.

SALINITY

The intrusion of salt into the soil—either from arid conditions or contamination of the water supply—is a real concern for most subtropical and tropical locations. Salt buildup occurs in arid soils due to the lack of precipitation and organic matter. Coastal regions are also affected when neighboring bodies of water leach salts into the ground, which affects the water supply. Salt spray is another concern when the sea is rough and winds blow over the water.

When saline soils are a problem, apply a three-inch layer of organic mulch to act as a buffer and install salt-tolerant plants. If your property snuggles up against a salt-water canal, river, or ocean, planting a salt-tolerant hedgerow will protect the more sensitive vegetation in the foreground. Place this buffer on the side where the wind and salt spray prevail, as it will protect the rest of the garden, as well the house, from salt spray.

PLANTING

Arizona, California, and Florida generally have poor soils with little organic matter. Amending alkaline or poor soils before planting is essential, unless you're using indigenous plants. When planting most shrubs, add at least two parts well-rotted manure or compost to one part native soil. Manure not only decreases the soil's pH, it creates a desirable environment for earthworms and beneficial microorganisms, retains soil moisture, increases soil fertility, decreases harmful nematodes, and turns local soil into a rich loam. Add a slow-release fertilizer and bone meal according to the manufacturer's instructions and mix well. Select a slow-release food that is high in potash (e.g., 5-5-10). Potash is the third number on fertilizer labels and is responsible for stimulating root growth and hardiness.

Water the plant the day before you transplant it into the ground to reduce transplant shock and to keep the root ball intact. Dig the hole before prying the plant out of its nursery container. The hole should be at least twice the width of the root ball and 6 to 12 inches deeper. The plant's crown—the junction where the roots and stem meet— should be even with the soil surface. Buried crowns often rot, and crowns

Digging may be back-breaking work if the soil is compacted and rocky.

planted too high have exposes roots, which dries them out. Pack the roots firmly into the soil, making sure there are no air pockets, then water well. Water every day or every other day, depending on the weather, for a couple of weeks. New growth indicates that the shrub has taken, after which you should water once or twice per week as necessary.

For azaleas, gardenias, ixoras, and other acid-loving plants, amend the soil by combining three or more parts compost or manure to two parts peat moss and one part native soil. When the surrounding soil is too alkaline for acid-loving plants, make the hole at least three times wider than the root ball. When planting more than one acid-loving shrub, group them together in their own bed. Amending an entire bed instead of each individual planting hole reduces contamination from the surrounding alkaline soil. Add at least three inches of organic mulch over the area to help retain the acidic conditions and to improve growing conditions. Replenish the mulch as necessary so it always remains at least three inches deep.

Amending soil is easy if the soil is sandy and loose, but it is back-breaking work where there is rock, compacted soil, or clay. Some areas in Hawaii have volcanic rock instead of soil, which makes amending soil, planting, and transplanting virtually impossible. If you can't dig down, consider raised beds or containers.

DRAINAGE

Good soil drainage is critical for most plants, unless they prefer bog or aquatic conditions. Persistent puddling is a sign that an area is too low, the soil is compacted, or a large underground obstruction is impairing drainage. If the problem is too difficult or impossible to fix, consider putting in raised beds, planting in containers, or converting the area to a bog garden or a pond. It is always easier to work with nature rather than against it.

If drainage is poor, consider working with Mother Nature and build a pond.

119

MULCH

Pine needles, coconut hulls, fir bark, redwood chips, eucalyptus, and other organic mulches are essential for healthy plant growth. Mulch reduces weeds, prevents soil erosion, lessens harmful nematodes, insulates the soil from temperature extremes, encourages beneficial soil microorganisms, increases

Organic mulch is beneficial for both plants and soil.

moisture retention, buffers the effects of salt contamination, and looks much better than bare soil. Place at least three inches of mulch on top of the soil and around plants, but keep it away from plant stems as it may cause rotting. Add new mulch on top of the old so it is always at least three inches deep.

FERTILIZING

Hungry tropical plants suffer more from environmental stresses such as cold temperatures, drought, flooding, and frost than healthy, well-fed specimens. Plants in areas with abundant rainfall and porous, sandy soil need frequent feedings. Southern Florida is prone to heavy rains during the summer, so nutrients are

This ixora is hungry and needs to be fertilized.

constantly flushed from the soil. Plant starvation is the norm and regular feeding must be maintained. To keep plants happy and well-fed, fertilize at least three times a year—in March, June, and October—with a slow-release, quality plant food that contains secondary elements and micronutrients. Use slow-release palm fertilizers, which are low in phosphorus and high in potash, for most shrubs. Phosphorus is generally not needed in large quantities since, unlike nitrogen and potash, it's retained in the soil. Most palm foods also contain micronutrients and secondary elements essential for a well-balanced diet. For acid-loving shrubs, use azalea and camellia fertilizers, which are specifically designed for acid-loving plants.

It's never a good idea to fertilize a plant when it's thirsty as it greedily absorbs the nutrients, which leads to fertilizer burn. Water the day before applying plant food, especially if plants are wilting from thirst. Apply fertilizer by broadcasting to at least a couple of feet beyond the plant's drip line, which is where the leaf canopy ends. Keep fertilizer granules away from trunks and stems, which may be burned by them. Always water well after applying granular plant food.

In arid regions, such as Arizona and California, salt accumulation due to over-fertilization is a common problem. Without adequate rainfall, the salts in fertilizers are not leached out of or dispersed throughout the soil. Instead they linger and build up to toxic levels. In areas with little rain, avoid feeding plants that are growing well and not showing deficiencies. Salt buildup is usually not a problem in wetter areas unless fertilizers are applied with a heavy hand.

If you must fertilize, remember that applying too much fertilizer at once causes the roots to burn as the salts draw moisture from the roots. Symptoms of fertilizer burn are brown leaf tips and scorched and distorted growth, usually followed by death. Reduce the chances of burning and provide a slow and steady dose of nutrients by using slow-release plant foods.

Although the use of too much fertilizer is a problem for arid areas, plants still may be deficient in trace and secondary elements. Foliar feedings are an efficient and safe way to deal with these deficiencies. If plants are hungry and yellow, apply nutritional sprays. Nutritional sprays are usually used for citrus plants and palms, but they are a great tonic for all plants. They contain essential micronutrients and secondary elements, such as manganese, magnesium, and iron, that are essential for plant health. They can be used any time of year to combat deficiencies and or to give plants a quick pick-me-up. Liquid nutritional sprays are mixed with water, then sprayed on the plants. Add a few drops of dishwashing liquid or use a sticker spreader to help the solution adhere to the foliage, which quickly absorbs the nutrients. The granular equivalent is sold as trace elements and is sprinkled on the ground, worked in, then irrigated. It takes longer for the nutrients to affect the plant, but it lasts longer than the liquid form.

Slow-release fertilizers are one of the best inventions known to gardeners. No matter what soil type you have, it is always better to provide a slow and steady flow of nutrients rather than a potent blast a few times a year. Quality is another important factor in fertilizer selection. It should contain iron, manganese, magnesium, and other micronutrients and secondary elements, so check fertilizer labels before your buy.

When it comes to the right product for your location, it is best to consult with your local horticultural experts. Neighborhood nurseries and university extension agencies know which fertilizers to use and when. Since each area of subtropical and tropical America has different soils and conditions, it is wise to find out which ones are suitable and recommended for your area.

JACK FROST

Although tropical and subtropical regions boast warm temperatures, frost is not unknown there. During December, January, and February, Jack Frost may arrive to take a tropical vacation. Adding high nitrogen fertilizer from November until March is not a good idea. Nitrogen promotes tender, lush growth, which is susceptible to frost damage.

The brown discoloration on this 'Silver Dwarf Discovery' allamanda shows tissue damage from cold temperatures.

Water plants during the day if frost is predicted that night. Avoid watering in the evening of the frost, as the water will freeze on the foliage, resulting in winterkill. During the winter months, it is a good idea to have burlap, old sheets, tablecloths, cardboard boxes, and other porous materials on hand to cover plants during cold weather. Avoid using plastic as it has little insulating value and suffocates plants. Wrap the material around the plants numerous times, making sure it touches the ground. Remove the cover during the day once the risk of frost has passed so cold air isn't trapped near the plant. This also gives the shrubs their daily share of air and sunlight. Don't forget to rewrap before nightfall if Jack decides to call again.

Making Plants Flower

One of the important things to remember when waiting for a shrub to flower is to be patient. Most shrubs take time to bloom after being planted. Sometimes it may take a few years for them gain enough stamina to develop flowers. Even if you bought a plant dripping with blossoms, it must grow new roots into the surrounding soil

Hibiscus plants flower freely unless their spot is too shady or they are being pruned too often.

and adjust to its new environment before blooming again. If a plant is reluctant to flower a year after planting, apply a fertilizer low in nitrogen, (which promotes lush, green foliage but doesn't stimulate flower production) and high in phosphorus or potash to promote flowering. Suitable fertilizers have high second or third numbers and a low first number (e.g., 2-8-4, 2-4-8).

Inadequate sunlight is another reason that many tropical specimens refuse to flower. If they are not receiving adequate light, they will also look spindly and be prone to fungus. Make sure sun worshippers receive at least eight hours of direct sun every day.

Plants that are cut back at the wrong time of the year may also fail to flower since this removes potential flower buds. Generally, prune just after a plant has finished flowering. For flora that rarely take a rest and are always in blossom, clip them back in spring and again in fall, but only if they need it. Avoid pruning from November to March because this promotes new growth, which is easily killed by freezing temperatures.

Pruning

Although pruning initially removes growth, it encourages new foliage and stems. After pruning, dormant buds along naked stems awaken, sprouting new leaves and branches. Generally, once a stem is severed, it usually develops two shoots at the place where it was cut. The extra branches and foliage turn a spindly shrub into a full and lush specimen.

123

Many tropical shrubs become leggy. Hibiscus and many other fast-growing specimens refuse to branch out, and their flowers end up being perched atop long, scrawny stems. Other plants naturally lose their lower leaves, resulting in bare stems. Careful pruning stimulates new growth and causes naked branches to produce foliage, converting an ugly duckling into a swan.

A hibiscus plant before being pruned.

Pruning increases the amount of flowers since it increases the number of branches. Pruning also generally encourages flowering. This isn't a hard and fast rule, however. In fact, if not done at the right time, pruning may hinder blossoming since most shrubs produce flowers on new growth. If new growth is removed, the plant is unable to blossom. In general, the best time to cut back flowering shrubs is right after they have finished flowering.

Since most tropical shrubs grow with gusto, it is tempting to cut them back severely, but it's not a good practice. Generally, remove one third of growth from a plant at a time. Shearing any shrub down to mere nubs saps the plant of its strength. It becomes susceptible to environmental stress and prone to insects and diseases. If a plant needs to be pruned often to keep it in check, it should be transplanted to a more appropriate location. To reduce the size of overgrown shrubs, remove one third in spring, summer, and fall. This is an effective and safe way to tame tropical giants without killing

The same plant after being pruned correctly.

them or turning them into deformed mutants.

Not all shrubs need to be pruned. If they are lush, full, healthy, and not in anyone's way, leave them alone. Just prune the ones that are spindly, overgrown, and lethargic. Many shrubs prefer to be pruned in spring, just before the buds break with new growth. Even evergreen plants develop new foliage during spring as they lose their old, tired leaves. Prune flowering plants after they finish flowering. Avoid pruning from November to March since frost may damage new leaves and buds.

This poor hibiscus has been pruned too severely. It will take a long time for it to recover and display its magnificent blooms.

Remove dead, diseased, broken, old, and unproductive stems any time of the year. Not only does this growth look unsightly, it promotes decay, disease, and insects. Remove crossing branches that rub together. The constant friction eventually causes the limbs to snap in half, which could be dangerous when you're dealing with large shrubs.

Eliminate growth that grows towards the center of the plant. Inward-growing stems and

When cutting back a stem, cut just above a node.

twigs deprive the plant's center of air and light, which causes the inside of the shrub to thin and decay.

To encourage stems to grow away from the plant's center, cut the branches to a bud or leaf that faces away from inside the shrub. All stems bear nodes, which are little bumps or scars located along their length. Flower buds, leaves, and even branches sprout from these unassuming blemishes. Always cut just above a node. If you sever the stem between nodes or just underneath one, a stub is created. The stub will die to at least the first node and sometimes further, taking the whole branch with it.

HEALTHY PLANTS

The tropics and subtropics are no stranger to insect pests and diseases. Since there's rarely a frost to kill these nasties, they linger from year to year. Each area of the tropical United States has different problems to deal with; plant maladies vary depending on the climate as well as the type of plant. Southern Florida and Hawaii are humid and wet, so fungus, rot, and molds are a constant battle. Southern Arizona and California have drier climates. Diseases aren't such a problem in these areas, although they do exist.

Healthy plants are tough and are able to naturally fight infection and infestations. When a plant is ill because it was planted in the wrong spot or is being neglected, it succumbs to insects and disease. To reduce infection and the spread of diseases, remove dead, dying, and broken limbs and other plant parts as soon as possible. Check the garden and plants daily to keep on top of problems. If a shrub is not happy in its current location and shows its displeasure by becoming sickly, it's a good idea to move it to a more suitable spot rather than fighting a losing battle.

Sometimes it is difficult to figure out if an insect or a fungus is responsible for plant damage. Generally, fungus appears as black and brown spots or white powder on foliage. Other symptoms include rotting, mushy, moist plant parts; wilting; and toadstools. If the fungus isn't controlled, plants succumb and die. Insect damage is easier to detect and control. Infestations generally appear as chewed, distorted, curled, and mottled growth.

When plants need to be treated, spray them thoroughly. Spray underneath foliage; on stems and branches; in nooks and crannies; and on surrounding soil. Reapply according to the manufacturer's instructions until there is no sign of further infection or infestation. Don't expect marred leaves and stems to miraculously regain their health after they have been sprayed. Once the tissue is damaged, it generally doesn't repair itself, but it does grow new parts. Healthy new growth is a sign that all is well and your treatments have been effective.

Years ago, chemical solutions to garden problems were unheard of. Gardeners and farmers alike turned to age-old methods of prevention and simple cures. Eventually technology gave us both good and bad products. Today, the use of these synthetic, toxic chemicals is becoming less popular due to the harmful effects on the environment and our health. However, pathogens and harmful insects continue to persist. Now technology again promises a bright future by offering bio-rational products to protect plants and the environment. Bio-rational pesticides are relatively non-toxic and have few ecological side effects. Generally, these include botanicals, microbial products, and minerals. Botanical bio-rational products are derived from plants such as rotenone, pyrethrum, sabadilla, and ryania. Microbial types are formulated from microorganisms such as *Bacillus thuringiensis*. Mineral bio-rational products include sulfur, copper, and potassium. When it comes to ridding the garden of harmful pests and diseases, reach for the bio-rational products instead of the toxic, synthetic chemicals of yesteryear.

INSECTS

Insects are part of nature so it is unrealistic to expect an insect-free garden. Besides, not all insects are bad. Many pollinate flowers, producing fruit and seeds. Others prey on bad insects that feast on our shrubs. A few unfavorable insects here and there are no big deal, but big infestations are. Thankfully, organic, bio-rational products such as horticultural oils, botanicals, and insecticidal soaps con-

Ladybugs are beneficial insects that devour aphids. The large insect to the left of the ladybug is a ladybug larva.

trol most insects. Thuricide (*Bacillus thuringiensis*) is a microbial insecticide that kills only caterpillars and is harmless to humans, pets, and beneficial organisms. It is extremely effective, but use care when using this product near butterfly gardens for obvious reasons.

There are two methods to control insects on plants: contact and systemic. Most organic and inorganic insecticides kill on contact, which means they have to touch the insects in order to kill them. Organocide, Ultra Fine Oil, and Safer's Insecticidal Soap are very effective, organic, contact controls. Malathion and Sevin are inorganic contact insecticides, and they are more toxic than their organic counterparts. Most insects—but not all—are successfully controlled by contact insecticides.

Dragonflies are beneficial insects that eat midges, mosquitoes, and other flying insects.

Systemic insecticides are suitable for hard-to-kill insects that protect themselves by hiding in the foliage or by feeding only at night. Some bugs, such as leaf miner and leaf roller caterpillars, use the leaves as protection. Leaf

An oleander caterpillar.

miners tunnel between the tissues of the leaf, and leaf rollers roll the foliage around themselves so they are shielded from predators. Other bugs come out only at night to feed and are nowhere to be seen during the day. Systemic insecticides control these sly pests in an insidious way. The chemical is absorbed by the plant via a foliar application or as a soil drench. The insecticide travels throughout the entire plant; the insect gets a mouthful of poison every time it takes a bite and ultimately dies.

Systemic insecticides are also handy for tenacious, hard-to-kill critters like scale insects and whiteflies. Scale insects are persistent, reproduce with gay abandon, and hang on for dear life, while whiteflies flit off as soon as you start to spray a contact insecticide. Systemics are not for all plants and conditions, however. They are very toxic and must be used with great care. Don't use them on edibles since the plants' edible parts—and, eventually, you—will also absorb the poison. If you don't wish to use systemics for obvious reasons, either live with imperfect plants or select ones that don't succumb to hard-to-control insects.

Scale insects on the underside of a false aralia leaf.

Scale insects on a gardenia.

Repeat applications are imperative for both systemic and contact insecticides to be effective. Insects produce hundreds of offspring (Aphids are even born pregnant!). Most contact insecticides should be reapplied every seven to ten days. Reapply systemics according to the manufacturer's instructions. Generally, insecticides do not prevent insects from feeding on

Aphids congregate on a rose bud.

plants. In fact, applying them too frequently actually promotes bad insects since the good guys that feed on the bad ones are also killed. Mother Nature needs a hand now and then, but avoid overspraying and allow her to do her thing.

DISEASES

Many plants survive insect damage, but surviving a disease is another story. Insects chew up the leaves or suck the juices out of a plant, but diseases spread throughout a plant's system, destroying its tissues and vascular system. It is important to act fast once a fungus, such as rot, mold, mildew, leaf spot, and wilt attacks. Remove and discard all dead and diseased plant parts as soon as they appear. Toss any shrub that's losing the battle so the infection doesn't carry throughout the garden to other plants.

Aphids clustered along the stem of this gardenia are responsible for the black, sooty mold on this leaf.

Unsuitable growing conditions are the usual culprit in a fungal infection. This is why it is so important to grow the

Black spot on azaleas is a common problem in humid places.

right plant in the right place. Crepe myrtles and other shrubs prone to powdery mildew should not sit under trees or dripping eaves. Grow fungus-prone, sun-loving plants where they will receive at least eight hours of direct sun a day beginning in the morning. Sun during first light evaporates the morning dew quickly so the fungus spores don't have a chance to germinate.

Another source of disease is soggy soil that doesn't drain quickly. Most shrubs prefer good drainage. Bad drainage is good only for bog and pond plants. In waterlogged soil, roots drown and rot, resulting in a foul odor and a mushy plant. Air circulation is another critical factor most people overlook when planting. Structures and overcrowded plants prohibit air circulation, creating stagnant air pockets. Space plants appropriately, keeping in mind their mature width. Avoid privacy fences and other structures that don't allow wind and light to enter and disperse throughout the garden. Instead, select fences that have offset or open slats.

Cleanliness is a crucial factor in disease control. Spores on fallen, contaminated leaves, flowers, buds, stems, twigs, and even the surrounding soil reinfest the host plant and infest neighboring ones. Be sure to also remove plagued, dead, decaying, and broken plant parts before spraying. Contaminated hands and tools also spread disease. Wash your hands and disinfect tools with bleach and water after touching an infected plant. Cleaning up debris not only reduces infection, it makes the garden aesthetically pleasing.

Powdery mildew on a crepe myrtle appears as a white powder that distorts the foliage.

Most diseases are controlled effectively with a copper-based fungicide, which is a bio-rational, mineral-based product. Use care when spraying a copper-based fungicide near concrete or stucco, as it will stain. Sulfur is another excellent organic fungicide effective in treating rusts and powdery mildew. Don't use sulfur in conjunction with horticultural oil insecticides or when the temperature is above 85° , however, as it may damage plant tissue.

Inorganic fungicides such as Daconil, Bayleton, and Funginex are also effective, but they should be used with care. Avoid using them used around ponds where there are fish and wildlife. Repeat applications are needed for both inorganic and organic fungicides according to the manufacturer's instructions.

Unlike insecticides, which don't prevent insects from feasting on plants, fungicides can be used preventatively to ward off disease. Copper-based fungicides are effective weapons when used once a month in humid, moist areas prone to diseases, such as southern Florida.

A WORD OF CAUTION

No matter what product you are using to fight insects, diseases, or weeds, it is important to be careful. Close your house and car windows before spraying, and wear long sleeves, long pants, closed shoes, a hat, glasses, and protective gloves. Don't spray on a windy day or when rain is predicted. Wash your clothes separately as soon as you have finished, then take a shower. Most people are careful when spraying non-organic products, especially ones that are systemic, but many organic controls may be toxic and must also be used with care.

Avoid treating plants at midday, especially if they are in full sun. Apply chemicals either early in the morning or late in the day. Oftentimes, inorganic and organic chemicals cause tissue damage (phytotoxicity) such as burning, leaf curl, and sometimes defoliation. Most pesticides and fungicides should not be applied at certain temperatures. Some products should not be combined with others, such as horticultural oils and fungicides. Many chemicals should not be used on certain plants, such as Malathion on hibiscus. Read the labels of all products and follow the instructions before doing the job, for your safety as well as the plant's.

SHRUB CLASSIFICATIONS

This section is designed to assist you in selecting the correct plants for your needs. It lists the shrubs described in the book by grouping together the ones that perform the same function or have similar characteristics. For example, if you're looking for a plant that grows to 4', flowers all year, and tolerates full sun, check within each specific category or subcategory (Mature Heights/Small Shrubs Up to 4', Shrubs That Flower Year-round, Sun and Shade Tolerance/Full Sun) to find one that is included in all three lists. The dwarf ixora turns up in each list. To make sure it's not invasive, check under Invasive Shrubs. The next step is to read the description of the plant in the Shrub Encyclopedia to find out more about it and decide if you like it.

MATURE HEIGHTS
These are the mature, non-pruned heights.

SMALL SHRUBS UP TO 4'

Bougainvillea – dwarf bougainvillea
Calliandra emarginata –
  dwarf powderpuff
Carissa macrocarpa –
  dwarf natal plum
Cordyline – Baby Ti
Dracaena sanderana – ribbon plant
Gardenia jasminoides radicans –
  dwarf gardenia
Ilex vomitoria – Stokes Dwarf
  holly
Ixora – Petite Red and
  Petite Pink ixoras
Ixora hybrid – Maui
Justicia – most species
Lagerstroemia – dwarf crepe myrtles
Malpighia coccigera – Singapore holly
Malpighia punica – Dwarf Pink
  Mound Singapore holly
Nerium oleander 'Petite' –
  dwarf oleander
Pachystachys lutea – golden shrimp
Pittosporum tobira – Wheeler's Dwarf
  pittosporum
Pseuderanthemum laxiflorum –
  shooting star shrub
Rhaphiolepis indica – dwarf Indian
  hawthorn
Rhododendron vireya – vireya
  rhododendron
Rosa – miniature roses
Russelia – firecracker plant
Ruttyruspolia – rutty
Strelitzia reginae – bird of paradise

MEDIUM SHRUBS FROM 4' TO 10'

Acalypha hispida – chenille plant
Acalypha wilkesiana –
  Picotee acalypha
Allamanda schottii – bush allamanda
Barleria cristata – Philippine violet
Bauhinia galpinii –
  nasturtium bauhinia
Breynia disticha – snowbush
Brunfelsia pauciflora 'Floribunda'–
  yesterday-today-and-tomorrow
Caesalpinia pulcherrima –
  dwarf poinciana
Calliandra – most species
Carissa macrocarpa – natal plum
Cestrum aurantiacum –
  yellow cestrum
Chrysobalanus icaco – Hobe Sound
  Dwarf cocoplum
Clerodendron bungei –
  cashmere bouquet
Clerodendron – most species
Codiaeum – croton
Cordyline – ti plant
Datura – devil's trumpet
Dracaena deremensis – dracaena
Dracaena fragrans – corn plant
Eranthemum pulchellum – blue sage
Euphorbia pulcherrima – poinsettia
Galphimia – thryallis
Gardenia jasminoides – gardenia
Gardenia thunbergia –
  thunbergia gardenia
Gossypium – wild cotton
Graptophyllum pictum –
  caricature plant
Hamelia cuprea – Bahama firebush
Hamelia patens 'African' –
  African firebush

Holmskioldia – Chinese hat plant
Ilex vomitoria 'Nana' –
     Nana dwarf holly
Ilex vomitoria 'Schillings' –
     Schillings dwarf holly
Ixora coccinea –
     Flame of the Woods ixora
Ixora hybrid – Nora Grant ixora
Jasminium multiflorum –
     downy jasmine
Jasminium nitidium – shining jasmine
Jatropha integerrima – most varieties
Justicia betonica – white shrimp
Lagerstroemia – dwarf crepe myrtle
Leucophyllum frutescens - Texas sage
Ligustrum sinense – Chinese privet
Loropetalum chinense – Chinese fringe
Manihot esculenta –
     variegated tapioca
Medinilla – most species
Mussaenda incana –
     yellow mussaenda
Odontonema strictum – firespike
Plumbago – most varieties
Polyscias – most aralia species
Psychotria nervosa – wild coffee
Rhaphiolepis indica –
     Indian hawthorn
Rhododendron – azalea
Rosa – most roses
Sanchezia – most species
Schefflera arboricola –
     dwarf schefflera
Senna (Cassia) alata – candle bush
Tabernaemontana divaricata 'Flore
     Pleno' – crepe jasmine
Tabernaemontana divaricata 'Pinwheel'
     – pinwheel jasmine
Tecomaria capensis –
     cape honeysuckle
Thunbergia erecta – king's mantle
Tibouchina urvilleana –
     princess flower

Viburnum suspensum –
     Sandankwa viburnum

TALL SHRUBS FROM 10'
Acalypha wilkesiana 'Ceylon' –
     fire dragon copperleaf
Acalypha wilkesiana 'Java White'–
     Java white acalypha
Acca (Feijoa) sellowiana –
     pineapple guava
Bougainvillea – bougainvillea
Brugmansia – angel trumpet
Calliandra haematocephala –
     powderpuff
Cestrum nocturnum –
     night-blooming jasmine
Chrysobalanus icaco – cocoplum
Clerodendrum speciosissimum –
     glory bower
Conocarpus erectus var. sericeus –
     silver buttonwood
Cryptostegia madagascariensis –
     Madagascar rubber vine
Dombeya – most species
Dracaena draco – dragon tree
Dracaena marginata –
     red margined dracaena
Dracaena reflexa – reflexed dracaena
Duranta erecta – golden dewdrop
Eugenia uniflora – Surinam cherry
Euphorbia pulcherrima – poinsettia
Gardenia taitensis – Tahitian gardenia
Hamelia patens – firebush
Hibiscus
Ilex vomitoria – yaupon holly
Ixora casei 'Super King' –
     'Super King' ixora
Jatropha integerrima –
     peregrina jatropha
Jatropha multifida – coral plant
Lagerstroemia – crepe myrtle
Ligustrum japonicum – Japanese privet
Malvaviscus arboreus – Turk's cap

Megaskepasma erythrochlamys –
   Brazilian red cloak
Murraya paniculata –
   orange jessamine
Mussaenda – most species
Nerium – oleander
Pittosporum tobira – pittosporum
Podocarpus macrophyllus –
   yew pine
Rosa – climbing roses
Schefflera (Dizygotheca) elegantissima –
   false aralia

Senna (Cassia) bicapsularis – cassia
Strelitzia nicolai –
   white bird of paradise
Tecoma stans – yellow elder
Tibouchina urvilleana –
   princess flower
Viburnum odoratissimum –
   most varieties
Vitex trifolia 'Variegata' –
   variegated vitex

MAINTAINABLE HEIGHTS

*The majority of shrubs are easily maintained at shorter
heights. The following subcategories list the average
heights at which shrubs are often kept.*

MAINTAINABLE HEIGHT TO 2'

Bougainvillea – dwarf bougainvillea
Calliandra emarginata –
   dwarf powderpuff
Calliandra haematocephala 'Nana' –
   Nana dwarf powderpuff
Carissa macrocarpa –
   dwarf natal plum
Chrysobalanus icaco – Hobe Sound
   Dwarf cocoplum
Codiaeum variegatum –
   Mammey croton
Cordyline – Baby Ti
Dracaena sanderana – ribbon plant
Euphorbia pulcherrima – poinsettia
Gardenia jasminoides radicans –
   dwarf gardenia
Ilex vomitoria – Nana and Stokes
   Dwarf yaupon holly
Ixora – 'Petite Red', 'Petite Pink'
Ixora hybrid – Maui ixora
Justicia – most species
Lagerstroemia – dwarf crepe myrtles
Leucophyllum frutescens – Texas sage
Malpighia coccigera – Singapore holly

Malpighia punica – Dwarf Pink
   Mound Singapore holly
Medinilla
Odontonema strictum – firespike
Pachystachys lutea – golden shrimp
Pittosporum tobira – most varieties
Plumbago auriculata – most varieties
Polyscias – most species
Pseuderanthemum laxiflorum –
   shooting star shrub
Psychotria nervosa – wild coffee
Rhaphiolepis indica – Indian
   hawthorn
Rosa – depending on the species
   and variety
Schefflera arboricola – dwarf
   schefflera
Thunbergia erecta – king's mantle
Viburnum suspensum – Sandankwa
   viburnum

MAINTAINABLE HEIGHT TO 4'

Acalypha hispida – chenille plant
Acalypha wilkesiana 'Picotee' – picotee acalypha

Allamanda schottii – bush allamanda
Barleria cristata – Philippine violet
Bauhinia galpinii –
    nasturtium bauhinia
Breynia disticha – snowbush
Brunfelsia pauciflora 'Floribunda' –
    yesterday-today-and-tomorrow
Calliandra haematocephala –
    powderpuff
Carissa grandiflora – natal plum
Cestrum aurantiacum –
    yellow cestrum
Chrysobalanus icaco –
    Red Tip cocoplum
Clerodendrum ugandense –
    blue clerodendrum
Codiaeum – croton
Conocarpus erectus var. sericeus –
    silver buttonwood
Cordyline – ti plant
Datura – devil's trumpet
Dracaena – most species
Eranthemum pulchellum – blue sage
Eugenia uniflora – Surinam cherry
Galphimia gracilus – thryallis
Gardenia jasminoides – gardenia
Gossypium hirsutum – wild cotton
Graptophyllum pictum –
    caricature plant
Hamelia – firebush
Hibiscus
Holmskioldia sanguinea –
    Chinese hat plant
Ilex vomitoria – Schillings Dwarf and
    Stokes Dwarf yaupon holly
Ixora – most species
Jasminium multiflorum –
    downy jasmine
Jasminium nitidium – shining jasmine
Jatropha integerrima 'Dwarf Jatropha'
    – dwarf peregrina
Justicia betonica – white shrimp
Justicia brandegeana – pink shrimp

Lagerstroemia – dwarf crepe myrtle
Loropetalum chinense – Chinese fringe
Murraya paniculata –
    orange jessamine
Mussaenda – most species
Nerium oleander 'Petite' –
    dwarf oleander
Odontonema strictum – firespike
Pittosporum – most species
Plumbago auriculata – most varieties
Podocarpus macrophyllus – yew pine
Rhododendron indicum –
    Southern Indian azaleas
Rhododendron kurume – dwarf azalea
Rhododendron vireya –
    vireya rhododendron
Rosa – most species and varieties
Russelia – firecracker plant
Ruttyruspolia – rutty
Sanchezia – most species
Senna (Cassia) alata – candlebush
Tabernaemontana divaricata 'Pinwheel'
    – pinwheel jasmine
Viburnum odoratissimum – sweet
    viburnum

MAINTAINABLE HEIGHT
TO 6'
Acalypha wilkesiana – most varieties
Acca (Feijoa) sellowiana –
    pineapple guava
Bougainvillea – most varieties
Caesalpinia pulcherrima –
    dwarf poinciana
Calliandra haematocephala –
    powderpuff
Clerodendron – most species
Cryptostegia madagascariensis –
    Madagascar rubber vine
Duranta erecta – golden dewdrop
Gardenia taitensis – Tahitian gardenia
Jatropha integerrima – peregrina
    jatropha

Lagerstroemia – crepe myrtle
Ligustrum – privet
Malvaviscus arboreus – Turk's cap
Manihot esculenta 'Variegata' –
    variegated tapioca
Megaskepasma erythrochlamys –
    Brazilian red cloak
Russelia – firecracker plant
Schefflera (Dizygotheca) elegantissima –
    false aralia
Senna (Cassia) bicapsularis – cassia
Tabernaemontana divaricata 'Flore
    Pleno' – crepe jasmine
Tecoma stans – yellow elder
Tecomaria capensis –
    cape honeysuckle
Tibouchina urvilleana –
    princess flower

Vitex trifolia – variegated vitex

MAINTAINABLE HEIGHT TO 8'

Clerodendron – most species
Cestrum nocturnum – night blooming
    jasmine
Dracaena reflexa – reflexed dracaena
Gardenia thunbergia –
    thunbergia gardenia
Nerium – oleander
Tabernaemontana divaricata –
    crepe jasmine
Tibouchina urvilleana –
    princess flower

SUN AND SHADE TOLERANCE

SHADE

Breynia disticha – snowbush
Cordyline – ti plant
Dracaena deremensis – dracaena
Dracaena fragrans – corn plant
Dracaena sanderana – ribbon plant
Eranthemum pulchellum – blue sage
Ilex vomitoria – yaupon holly
Justicia carnea – flamingo flower
Medinella
Megaskepasma erythrochlamys –
    Brazillian red cloak
Polyscias – aralia
Psychotria nervosa – wild coffee
Rhododendron – azalea
Rhododendron vireya –
    vireya rhododendron
Schefflera arboricola – dwarf schefflera

PARTIAL SHADE

Acca (Feijoa) sellowiana –
    pineapple guava
Barleria cristata – Philippine violet

Breynia disticha – snowbush
Brugmansia – angel trumpet
Brunfelsia pauciflora 'Floribunda' –
    yesterday-today-and-tomorrow
Carissa – natal plum species
Cestrum aurantiacum –
    yellow cestrum
Clerodendrum – most species
Codiaeum variegatum – croton
Cordyline – ti plant
Datura – devil's trumpet
Dracaena deremensis – dracaena
Dracaena fragrans – corn plant
Dracaena sanderana – ribbon plant
Duranta erecta – golden dewdrop
Eranthemum pulchellum – blue sage
Eugenia uniflora – Surinam cherry
Graptophyllum pictum –
    caricature plant
Hamelia patens – firebush
Holmskioldia sanguinea –
    Chinese hat plant
Ilex vomitoria – yaupon holly

Jasminium – most species
Jatropha – most species
Ligustrum – privet
Loropetalum – Chinese fringe
Malpighia – most species
Manihot – most species
Medinella – most species
Megaskepasma erythrochlamys –
    Brazillian red cloak
Murraya paniculata –
    orange jessamine
Odontonema strictum – firespike
Pachystachys lutea –
    golden shrimp plant
Pittosporum tobira – most varieties
Plumbago auriculata – most varieties
Podocarpus macrophyllus – yew pine
Polyscias – aralia
Pseuderanthemum laxiflorum –
    shooting star shrub
Psychotria nervosa – wild coffee
Rhaphiolepis indica –
    Indian hawthorn
Sanchezia – most species
Schefflera (*Dizygotheca*) *elegantissima* –
    false aralia
Schefflera arboricola – aralia schefflera
Tabernaemontana – most species
Thunbergia erecta – king's mantle
Tibouchina urvilleana – princess
    flower
Viburnum – most species

FULL SUN

Acalypha hispida – chenille plant
Acalypha wilkesiana – most varieties
Acca (*Feijoa*) *sellowiana* –
    pineapple guava
Allamanda schottii – bush allamanda
Barleria cristata – Philippine violet
Bauhinia galpinii –
    nasturtium bauhinia

Bougainvillea – bougainvillea
Breynia disticha – snowbush
Brunfelsia pauciflora 'Floribunda' –
    yesterday-today-and-tomorrow
Caesalpinia pulcherrima –
    dwarf poinciana
Calliandra – powderpuff
Carissa – natal plum
Cestrum – most species
Chrysobalanus icaco – cocoplum
Clerodendrum – most species
Codiaeum – croton
Cryptostegia madagascariensis –
    Madagascar rubber vine
Dombeya – tropical snowball
Dracaena draco – dragon tree
Dracaena marginata –
    red-edged dracaena
Dracaena reflexa – reflexed dracaena
Duranta erecta – golden dewdrop
Eugenia uniflora – Surinam cherry
Euphorbia pulcherrima – poinsettia
Galphimia gracilus – thryallis
Gardenia
Gossypium hirsutum – wild cotton
Graptophyllum pictum –
    caricature plant
Hamelia patens – firebush
Hibiscus
Holmskioldia sanguinea –
    Chinese hat plant
Ilex vomitoria – yaupon holly
Ixora
Jasminium – jasmine
Jatropha – most species
Lagerstroemia – crepe myrtle
Leucophyllum frutescens – Texas sage
Ligustrum japonicum – Japanese privet
Loropetalum – Chinese fringe
Malpighia – Singapore holly
Malvaviscus arboreus – Turk's cap
Manihot – variegated tapioca

141

Murraya paniculata –
orange jessamine
Mussaenda
Nerium oleander – oleander
Pachystachys lutea – golden shrimp
Pittosporum
Plumbago
Podocarpus – yew pine
Polyscias – aralias
Pseuderanthemum –
shooting star shrub
Rhaphiolepis indica – Indian
hawthorn
Rosa – rose
Russelia – firecracker plant
Ruttyruspolia – rutty
Sanchezia – most species
Schefflera (*Dizygotheca*) *elegantissima* –
false aralia
Schefflera arboricola – aralia schefflera
Senna (*Cassia*) – most species
Strelitzia – bird of paradise
Tabernaemontana – most species
Tecoma stans – yellow elder
Tecomaria capensis –
cape honeysuckle
Thunbergia erecta – king's mantle
Viburnum
Vitex – most species

FULL SUN TO PARTIAL
SHADE

Acca (*Feijoa*) *sellowiana* –
pineapple guava
Barleria cristata – Philippine violet
Brunfelsia pauciflora 'Floribunda' –
yesterday-today-and-tomorrow
Carissa – natal plum
Cestrum aurantiacum –
yellow cestrum
Clerodendrum
Codiaeum – croton

Dracaena draco – dragon tree
Dracaena marginata –
red-edged dracaena
Dracaena reflexa – reflexed dracaena
Duranta erecta – golden dewdrop
Eugenia uniflora – Surinam cherry
Gardenia
Graptophyllum pictum –
caricature plant
Hamelia – firebush
Holmskioldia – Chinese hat plant
Ilex vomitoria – yaupon holly
Jasminium – jasmine
Jatropha integerrima –
peregrina jatropha
Ligustrum japonicum – Japanese privet
Loropetalum – Chinese fringe
Manihot – variegated tapioca
Murraya paniculata –
orange jessamine
Nerium – oleander
Pachystachys lutea –
golden shrimp plant
Pittosporum
Plumbago
Podocarpus macrophyllus – yew pine
Polyscias – aralia
Pseuderanthemum laxiflorum –
shooting star shrub
Rhaphiolepis indica –
Indian hawthorn
Sanchezia
Schefflera (*Dizygotheca*) *elegantissima* –
false aralia
Schefflera arboricola – dwarf schefflera
Tabernaemontana divaricata 'Flore
Pleno' – crepe jasmine
Tabernaemontana divaricata 'Pinwheel'
– pinwheel jasmine
Thunbergia erecta – king's mantle
Viburnum

Cordyline – ti plant
Dracaena deremensis – dracaena
Dracaena fragrans – corn plant
Dracaena sanderana – ribbon plant
Eranthemum pulchellum – blue sage
Graptophyllum pictum –
    caricature plant
Justicia carnea – flamingo flower
Medinella
Megaskepasma erythrochlamys –
    Brazillian red cloak

Psychotria nervosa – wild coffee
Schefflera arboricola –
    dwarf schefflera

SUN AND SHADE
Graptophyllum pictum – caricature plant
Ilex vomitoria – yaupon holly
Polyscias – aralias
Schefflera arboricola –
    dwarf schefflera

FRAGRANT SHRUBS

Acca (Feijoa) sellowiana –
    pineapple guava
Brugmansia – angel trumpet
Brunfelsia pauciflora 'Floribunda' –
    yesterday-today-and-tomorrow
Calliandra – powderpuff
Carissa – natal plum
Cestrum nocturnum –
    night blooming jasmine
Clerodendron bungei –
    cashmere bouquet
Datura – devil's trumpet
Dracaena fragrans – corn plant
Duranta erecta – golden dewdrop

Eugenia uniflora – Surinam cherry
Gardenia
Jasminium nitidum – shining jasmine
Ligustrum – privet
Loropetalum – Chinese fringe
Murraya paniculata –
    orange jessamine
Nerium – oleander
Pittosporum – most species
Rhaphiolepis indica –
    Indian hawthorn
Rosa – most varieties
Viburnum – most species

SHRUBS SUITABLE FOR SPECIMENS

Acalypha hispida – chenille plant
Acca (Feijoa) sellowiana –
    pineapple guava
Allamanda schottii – bush allamanda
Bougainvillea – bougainvillea
Breynia disticha – snowbush
Brugmansia – angel trumpet
Calliandra – powderpuff
Carissa – natal plum
Clerodendrum minahassae –
    tube flower
Clerodendrum myricoides 'Ugandense'

    – blue clerodendrum
Clerodendrum quadriloculare –
    starburst clerodendrum
Codiaeum – croton
Datura – devil's trumpet
Dombeya – tropical snowball
Dracaena reflexa – reflexed dracaena
Hamelia – firebush
Hibiscus
Ixora – most species
Jatropha integerrima –
    peregrina

jatropha
Jatropha multifida – coral plant
Lagerstroemia – crepe myrtle
Ligustrum – privet
Malvaviscus arboreus – Turk's cap
Megaskepasma erythrochlamys –
    Brazillian red cloak
Murraya paniculata –
    orange jessamine
Mussaenda
Odontonema strictum – firespike
Pachystachys lutea – golden shrimp
Polyscias – aralia

Rhododendron vireya –
    vireya rhododendron
Rosa – rose
Russelia – firecracker plant
Schefflera (Dizygotheca) elegantissima –
    false aralia
Tabernaemontana divaricata 'Flore
    Pleno' – crepe jasmine
Tabernaemontana divaricata 'Pinwheel'
    – pinwheel jasmine
Tecoma stans – yellow elder
Tibouchina urvilleana –
    princess flower

SHRUBS SUITABLE FOR ACCENTS

Acalypha hispida – chenille plant
Acalypha wilkesiana – most varieties
Acca (Feijoa) sellowiana –
    pineapple guava
Allamanda schottii – bush allamanda
Barleria cristata – Philippine violet
Bougainvillea – bougainvillea
Brunfelsia pauciflora 'Floribunda' –
    yesterday-today-and-tomorrow
Caesalpinia pulcherrima –
    dwarf poinciana
Calliandra – powderpuff
Carissa – natal plum
Chrysobalanus icaco – cocoplum
Clerodendrum minahassae –
    tube flower
Clerodendrum myricoides 'Ugandense'
    – blue clerodendrum
Clerodendrum quadriloculare –
    starburst clerodendrum
Codiaeum – croton
Conocarpus erectus var. sericeus –
    silver buttonwood
Cordyline – most species
Cryptostegia madagascariensis –
    Madagascar rubber vine
Datura – devil's trumpet

Dracaena – most species
Duranta erecta – golden dewdrop
Eranthemum pulchellum – blue sage
Euphorbia pulcherrima – poinsettia
Galphimia gracilus – thryallis
Gardenia
Gossypium hirsutum – wild cotton
Graptophyllum pictum –
    caricature plant
Hamelia patens– firebush
Hibiscus
Ixora – most species
Jatropha integerrima – peregrina
Jatropha multifida – coral plant
Justicia brandegeana – shrimp plant
Justicia carnea – flamingo flower
Lagerstroemia– crepe myrtle
Leucophyllum frutescens – Texas sage
Loropetalum – Chinese fringe
Malpighia coccigera – Singapore holly
Malvaviscus arboreus – Turk's cap
Manihot esculenta 'Variegata' –
    variegated tapioca
Medinilla
Murraya paniculata –
    orange jessamine
Mussaenda

Nerium oleander – oleander
Odontonema strictum – firespike
Pachystachys lutea – golden shrimp
Plumbago
Podocarpus macrophyllus –yew pine
Polyscias – aralia
Pseuderanthemum laxiflorum –
    shooting star shrub
Psychotria nervosa – wild coffee
Rhaphiolepis indica –
    Indian hawthorn
Rhododendron – azaleas
Rhododendron vireya –
    vireya rhododendron
Rosa – rose
Russelia – firecracker plant

Ruttyruspolia – rutty
Schefflera (Dizygotheca elegantissima) –
    false aralia
Schefflera arboricola – aralia schefflera
Senna (Cassia) – most species
Strelitzia – bird of paradise
Tabernaemontana divaricata 'Flore
    Pleno' – crepe jasmine
Tabernaemontana divaricata 'Pinwheel'
    – pinwheel jasmine
Tecoma stans – yellow elder
Thunbergia erecta – king's mantle
Tibouchina urvilleana –
    princess flower
Vitex trifolia 'Variegata' –
    variegated vitex

SHRUBS SUITABLE FOR FOUNDATION PLANTINGS

Acalypha hispida – chenille plant
Acalypha wilkesiana – most varieties
Acca (Feijoa) sellowiana –
    pineapple guava
Allamanda schottii – bush allamanda
Bougainvillea – dwarf bougainvillea
Breynia disticha – snowbush
Brunfelsia pauciflora 'Floribunda' –
    yesterday-today-and-tomorrow
Carissa – natal plum
Chrysobalanus icaco – cocoplum
Clerodendrum minahassae –
    tube flower
Clerodendrum myricoides 'Ugandense'
    – blue clerodendrum
Clerodendrum quadriloculare –
    starburst clerodendrum
Codiaeum – croton
Cordyline – ti plant
Dracaena
Duranta repens – golden dewdrop
Eranthemum pulchellum – blue sage
Eugenia uniflora – Surinam cherry
Galphimia gracilus – thryallis

Gardenia
Graptophyllum pictum –
    caricature plant
Hibiscus
Ilex vomitoria – dwarf yaupon holly
Ixora
Jatropha integerrima – peregrina
    jatropha and dwarf peregrina
Jatropha multifida – coral plant
Justicia – most species
Lagerstroemia – crepe myrtle
Leucophyllum frutescens – Texas sage
Ligustrum – privet
Loropetalum chinense – Chinese fringe
Malpighia – Singapore holly
Murraya paniculata –
    orange jessamine
Mussaenda
Nerium oleander 'Petite'–
    dwarf oleanders
Odontonema strictum – firespike
Pachystachys lutea –
    golden shrimp plant
Pittosporum tobira – most varieties

Plumbago
Podocarpus macrophyllus – yew pine
Polyscias – aralia
Pseuderanthemum laxiflorum –
　　shooting star shrub
Psychotria nervosa – wild coffee
Rhaphiolepis indica –
　　Indian hawthorn
Rhododendron – azaleas
Rhododendron vireya –
　　vireya rhododendron
Rosa – rose
Russelia – firecracker
Ruttyruspolia – rutty
Schefflera (Dizygotheca) elegantissima –
false aralia
Schefflera arboricola – aralia schefflera
Strelitzia reginae –
　　orange bird of paradise
Tabernaemontana divaricata 'Flore
　　Pleno' – crepe jasmine
Tabernaemontana divaricata 'Pinwheel'
　　– pinwheel jasmine
Thunbergia erecta – king's mantle
Tibouchina urvilleana –
　　princess flower
Viburnum – most species
Vitex trifolia 'Variegata' –
　　variegated vitex

SHRUBS SUITABLE FOR SCREENS

Acalypha wilkesiana – most varieties
Bougainvillea – bougainvillea
Caesalpinia pulcherrima –
　　dwarf poinciana
Calliandra – powderpuff
Carissa – natal plum
Chrysobalanus icaco – cocoplum
Clerodendron bungei –
　　cashmere bouquet
Clerodendrum paniculatum –
　　pagoda flower
Clerodendrum speciosissimum –
　　glory bower
Codiaeum – croton
Duranta repens – golden dewdrop
Eugenia uniflora – Surinam cherry
Gardenia – most species except
　　dwarfs
Graptophyllum pictum – caricature plant
Hamelia patens – firebush
Hibiscus
Holmskioldia – Chinese hat plant
Ixora – most species, except dwarfs
Ligustrum – privet
Malvaviscus arboreus – Turk's cap
Megaskepasma erythrochlamys –
　　Brazillian red cloak
Murraya paniculata –
　　orange jessamine
Nerium – oleander except dwarfs
Odontonema strictum – firespike
Podocarpus macrophyllus – yew pine
Strelitzia nicolai –
　　white bird of paradise
Rosa – China and tea roses
Sanchezia – most species
Tabernaemontana divaricata 'Flore
　　Pleno' – crepe jasmine
Tecomaria capensis –
　　cape honeysuckle
Thunbergia erecta – king's mantle
Viburnum
Vitex trifolia 'Variegata' –
　　variegated vitex

SHRUBS SUITABLE FOR BACKGROUNDS

Calliandra – powderpuff
Carissa – natal plum
Chrysobalanus icaco – cocoplum
Duranta erecta – golden dewdrop
Eugenia uniflora – Surinam cherry
Gardenia – except dwarfs
Hamelia patens – firebush
Holmskioldia sanguinea –
    Chinese hat plant
Ilex vomitoria – yaupon holly
Ligustrum – privet
Malvaviscus arboreus – Turk's cap
Megaskepasma erythrochlamys –
    Brazillian red cloak
Murraya paniculata – orange jasmine
Nerium – oleander
Odontonema strictum – firespike
Podocarpus macrophyllus –
    yew podocarpus
Psychotria nervosa – wild coffee
Strelitzia nicolai -
    white bird of paradise
Tabernaemontana divaricata 'Flore
    Pleno' – crepe jasmine
Thunbergia erecta – king's mantle
Viburnum – most species

SHRUBS SUITABLE FOR HEDGES
* (formal), ** (informal), or *** (either)

Acalypha wilkesiana –
    most varieties**
Acca (Feijoa) sellowiana –
    pineapple guava***
Barleria cristata – Philippine violet***
Bauhinia galpinii –
    nasturtium bauhinia**
Bougainvillea – bougainvillea**
Breynia disticha – snowbush***
Calliandra haematocephala –
    powderpuff***
Carissa – natal plum***
Chrysobalanus icaco – cocoplum***
*Clerodendrum**
Codiaeum – croton**
Duranta erecta – golden dewdrop**
Eugenia uniflora – Surinam cherry***
Galphimia gracilus – thryallis**
*Gardenia**
Graptophyllum pictum –
    caricature plant**
Hamelia patens – firebush**
*Hibiscus**
Ilex vomitoria – yaupon holly*
Ixora – most species***
Jasminium – jasmine***
Justicia brandegeana – shrimp plant**
Leucophyllum frutescens –
    Texas sage***
Ligustrum – privet***
Malpighia coccigera – Singapore
    holly*
Malvaviscus arboreus – Turk's cap**
Murraya paniculata –
    orange jasmine***
Nerium – oleander**
Odontonema strictum – firespike**
*Pittosporum tobira**
Plumbago **
Podocarpus macrophyllus – yew pine***
Polyscias – aralia***
Psychotria nervosa – wild coffee**
Rhaphiolepis indica –
    Indian hawthorn***
Rosa – China and tea roses**
Russelia – firecracker**
Ruttyruspolia – rutty**
Sanchezia – most species **
Schefflera arboricola –
    aralia schefflera**
Tabernaemontana divaricata 'Flore
    Pleno' – crepe jasmine**

Tabernaemontana divaricata 'Pinwheel'
  – pinwheel jasmine**
Tecomaria capensis – cape honeysuckle**
Thunbergia erecta – king's mantle***
Tibouchina urvilleana –
  princess flower**

Viburnum odoratissimum –
  sweet viburnum**
Viburnum suspensum –
  Sandankwa viburnum***
Vitex trifolia 'Variegata' –
  variegated vitex***

SHRUBS SUITABLE FOR BANK COVERS

Bauhinia galpinii –
  nasturtium bauhinia
Calliandra – powderpuff
Carissa – natal plum
Clerodendron bungei –
  cashmere bouquet
Holmskioldia – Chinese hat plant
Ilex vomitoria – yaupon holly
Jasminium – jasmine

Justicia brandegeana – shrimp plant
Megaskepasma erythrochlamys –
  Brazillian red cloak
Murraya paniculata – orange jasmine
Pittosporum tobira – most varieties
Plumbago
Russelia – firecracker plant
Tecomaria capensis –
  cape honeysuckle

SHRUBS SUITABLE AS SMALL TREES

Acca (Feijoa) sellowiana –
  pineapple guava
Bougainvillea – bougainvillea
Breynia disticha – snowbush
Brugmansia – angel trumpet
Dombeya – tropical snowball
Eugenia uniflora – Surinam cherry
Gossypium hirsutum – wild cotton
Hibiscus – most species and varieties
Ilex vomitoria – yaupon holly
Jatropha integerrima –
  peregrina jatropha
Jatropha multifida – coral plant
Lagerstroemia– crepe myrtle
Ligustrum – privet
Loropetalum – Chinese fringe
Murraya paniculata – orange jasmine

Nerium – oleander
Pittosporum tobira – most varieties
Podocarpus macrophyllus – yew pine
Polyscias – aralia
Rhododendron indica –
  Southern Indian azalea
Schefflera (Dizygotheca elegantissima) –
  false aralia
Schefflera arboricola – dwarf schefflera
Tabernaemontana divaricata 'Flore
  Pleno' – crepe jasmine
Tabernaemontana divaricata 'Pinwheel'
  – pinwheel jasmine
Tecoma stans – yellow elder
Vitex trifolia 'Variegata' –
  variegated vitex

SHRUBS SUITABLE FOR MASSING

Bauhinia galpinii –
nasturtium bauhinia
Bougainvillea – dwarf bougainvillea
Breynia disticha – snowbush
Calliandra – powderpuff
Carissa macrocarpa –
dwarf natal plum
Chrysobalanus icaco – cocoplum
Codiaeum variegatum –
Mammey croton
Eranthemum pulchellum – blue sage
Galphimia gracilus – thryallis
Gardenia – dwarf gardenia
Ilex vomitoria – dwarf yaupon holly
Ixora – most species
Jasminium – jasmine

Justicia carnea – flamingo flower
Loropetalum – Chinese fringe
Malpighia – Singapore holly
Nerium oleander 'Petites' –
dwarf oleander
Pittosporum tobira – most varieties
Plumbago
Psychotria nervosa – wild coffee
Rhaphiolepis indica – Indian
hawthorn
Rhododendron – azalea
Russelia – firecracker
Schefflera arboricola – dwarf schefflera
Viburnum suspensum –
Sandankwa viburnum

SHRUBS SUITABLE FOR CONTAINERS

Acalypha hispida – chenille plant
Bauhinia galpinii –
nasturtium bauhinia
Bougainvillea – bougainvillea
Breynia disticha – snowbush
Brugmansia – angel trumpet
Brunfelsia pauciflora 'Floribunda' –
yesterday-today-and-tomorrow
Carissa – natal plum
Chrysobalanus icaco – cocoplum
Codiaeum – croton
Cordyline – ti plant
Datura – devil's trumpet
Dombeya – tropical snowball
Dracaena – most species
Duranta erecta – golden dewdrop
Eranthemum pulchellum – blue sage
Euphorbia pulcherrima – poinsettia
Gardenia jasminoides – gardenia
Gossypium hirsutum – wild cotton
Graptophyllum pictum –
caricature plant
Hibiscus

Ilex vomitoria – dwarf yaupon holly
Ixora
Jasminium – jasmine
Jatropha integerrima –
peregrina jatropha
Jatropha multifida – coral plant
Justicia – most species
Lagerstroemia – crepe myrtle
Leucophyllum frutescens – Texas sage
Ligustrum – privet
Malpighia – Singapore holly
Manihot esculenta 'Variegata' –
variegated tapioca
Medinilla
Murraya paniculata –
orange jessamine
Mussaenda
Nerium oleander 'Petites' –
dwarf oleander
Pachystachys lutea – golden shrimp
Pittosporum
Plumbago
Podocarpus macrophyllus – yew pine

Polyscias – aralia
Pseuderanthemum laxiflorum –
   shooting star shrub
Psychotria nervosa – wild coffee
Rhaphiolepis indica –
   Indian hawthorn
Rhododendron – most species
Rosa – rose
Russelia – firecracker
Schefflera (Dizygotheca) elegantissima –
   false aralia
Schefflera arboricola – dwarf schefflera
Strelitzia reginae – bird of paradise
Tabernaemontana divaricata 'Pinwheel'
   – pinwheel jasmine
Tecoma stans – yellow elder
Thunbergia erecta – king's mantle
Viburnum suspensum –
   Sandankwa viburnum

SHRUBS SUITABLE FOR THE LANAI

Breynia disticha – snowbush
Chrysobalanus icaco – cocoplum
Cordyline – ti plant
Dracaena
Gardenia
Ilex vomitoria – dwarf yaupon holly
Malpighia – Singapore holly
Pittosporum
Polyscias – aralia
Rhaphiolepis indica –
   Indian hawthorn
Schefflera arboricola – dwarf schefflera

DROUGHT-TOLERANT SHRUBS

Acca (Feijoa) sellowiana –
   pineapple guava
Allamanda schottii – bush allamanda
Bougainvillea – bougainvillea
Caesalpinia pulcherrima –
   dwarf poinciana
Calliandra – powderpuff
Carissa – natal plum
Codiaeum – croton
Cordyline –ti plant
Cryptostegia madagascariensis –
   Madagascar rubber vine
Dracaena draco – dragon tree
Dracaena marginata – red-margined
   dracaena
Dracaena reflexa – reflexed dracaena
Dracaena sanderana – ribbon plant
Duranta repens – golden dewdrop
Gossypium hirsutum – wild cotton
Hamelia – firebush
Ilex vomitoria – yaupon holly
Jatropha integerrima –
   peregrina jatropha
Jatropha multifida – coral plant
Lagerstroemia– crepe myrtle
Leucophyllum frutescens – Texas sage
Ligustrum – privet
Malvaviscus arboreus – Turk's cap
Murraya paniculata –
   orange jessamine
Nerium – oleander
Pittosporum
Plumbago
Polyscias – aralia
Rhaphiolepis indica –
   Indian hawthorn
Russelia – firecracker
Schefflera arboricola –
   dwarf schefflera
Tecoma stans – yellow elder
Viburnum suspensum – Sandankwa
   viburnum

SHRUBS TOLERANT OF WET SOILS

Acalypha – most species
Dracaena – most species
Graptophyllum pictum –
    caricature plant

Hamelia patens – firebush

HIGH SALT–TOLERANT SHRUBS

Bougainvillea – bougainvillea
Carissa – natal plum
Chrysobalanus icaco – cocoplum
Dracaena draco – dragon tree
Gossypium hirsutum – wild cotton

Ilex vomitoria – yaupon holly
Nerium – oleander
Pittosporum
Podocarpus macrophyllus – yew pine
Russelia – firecracker

MEDIUM SALT–TOLERANT SHRUBS

Acalypha hispida – chenille plant
Acalypha wilkesiana – most varieties
Acca (Feijoa) sellowiana –
    pineapple guava
Allamanda schottii – bush allamanda
Brunfelsia pauciflora – yesterday-
    today-and-tomorrow
Caesalpinia pulcherrima –
    dwarf poinciana
Cestrum aurantiacum –
    yellow cestrum
Cestrum nocturnum –
    night blooming jasmine
Codiaeum – croton
Cryptostegia madagascariensis –
    Madagascar rubber vine
Duranta erecta – golden dewdrop
Eranthemum pulchellum – blue sage
Eugenia uniflora – Surinam cherry
Galphimia gracilus – thryallis
Hamelia – firebush
Hibiscus
Holmskioldia sanguinea –
    Chinese hat plant
Ixora
Jasminium nitidum – shining jasmine
Jatropha integerrima –
    peregrina jatropha
Jatropha multifida – coral plant

Leucophyllum frutescens – Texas sage
Ligustrum – privet
Malpighia coccigera – Singapore holly
Murraya paniculata –
    orange jessamine
Plumbago
Podocarpus macrophyllus – yew pine
Polyscias – aralia
Pseuderanthemum laxiflorum –
    shooting star shrub
Psychotria nervosa – wild coffee
Rhaphiolepis indica –
    Indian hawthorn
Sanchezia – most species
Schefflera (Dizygotheca elegantissima) –
    false aralia
Schefflera arboricola – dwarf schefflera
Senna (Cassia) – most species
Tabernaemontana divaricata 'Flore
    Pleno' – crepe jasmine
Tabernaemontana divaricata 'Pinwheel'
    – pinwheel jasmine
Tecoma stans – yellow elder
Tecomaria capensis –
    cape honeysuckle
Thunbergia erecta – king's mantle
Vitex trifolia 'Variegata' – variegated
    vitex

LOW SALT-TOLERANT SHRUBS

Barleria cristata – Philippine violet
Bauhinia galpinii –
    nasturtium bauhinia
Breynia disticha – snowbush
Brugmansia – angel trumpet
Calliandra – powderpuff
Clerodendrum – most species
Cordyline – ti plant
Datura – devil's trumpet
Dombeya – tropical snowball
Dracaena deremensis – dracaena
Dracaena draco – dragon tree
Dracaena fragrans – corn plant
Dracaena marginata –
    red-margined dracaena
Dracaena reflexa – reflexed dracaena
Dracaena sanderana – ribbon plant
Euphorbia pulcherrima – poinsettia
Gardenia
Graptophyllum pictum –
    caricature plant
Jasminium multiflorum –
    downy jasmine

Justicia betonica – white shrimp
Justicia brandegeana – shrimp plant
Justicia carnea – flamingo flower
Lagerstroemia – crepe myrtle
Loropetalum chinense – Chinese fringe
Malvaviscus arboreus – Turk's cap
Manihot esculenta 'Variegata' –
    variegated tapioca
Medinella – most species
Megaskepasma erythrochlamys –
    Brazillian red cloak
Mussaenda – most species
Odontonema strictum – firespike
Pachystachys lutea –
    golden shrimp plant
Rhododendron –
    azalea and rhododendron
Rosa – rose
Ruttyruspolia – rutty
Tibouchina urvilleana –
    princess flower
Viburnum – most species

INVASIVE SHRUBS

Breynia disticha – snowbush
Clerodendrum bungei –
    cashmere bouquet
Clerodendrum paniculatum –
    pagoda flower
Clerodendrum speciosissimum –
    Java glorybower
Eugenia uniflora –Surinam cherry
Ilex vomitoria – yaupon holly
Odontonema strictum – firespike

Pittosporum tobira – most varieties
Russelia equisetiformis –
    firecracker plant
Sanchezia – most species
Schefflera (Brassaia) actinophylla –
    Queensland umbrella tree
Schinus terebinthifolius –
    Brazilian pepper tree
Senna (Cassia) bicapsularis – cassia

SHRUBS FOR BUTTERFLY GARDENS

Calliandra haematocephala –
    red powderpuff
Cestrum aurantiacum –
    yellow cestrum

Clerodendron bungei –
    cashmere bouquet
Duranta erecta – golden dewdrop
Hamelia patens – firebush

Hibiscus
Odontonema strictum – firespike
Plumbago

Senna – cassia
Viburnum
Vitex

SHRUBS FOR BIRD GARDENS

Acca (Feijoa) sellowiana –
   pineapple guava
Calliandra – powderpuff
Cestrum aurantiacum –
   yellow cestrum
Chrysobalanus icaco – cocoplum
Duranta repens – golden dewdrop
Eugenia uniflora – Surinam cherry
Hamelia patens – firebush
Hibiscus
Jatropha integerrima –
   peregrine jatropha
Justicia brandegeana – shrimp plant

Leucophyllum frutescens – Texas sage
Malpighia – Singapore holly
Malvaviscus arboreus – Turk's cap
Murraya paniculata –
   orange jessamine
Odontonema strictum – firespike
Pachystachys lutea – golden shrimp
Podocarpus macrophyllus – yew pine
Polyscias – aralia
Psychotria nervosa – wild coffee
Rhaphiolepis indica –
   Indian hawthorn
Viburnum

SHRUBS THAT FLOWER YEAR-ROUND

Allamanda schottii – bush allamanda
Barleria cristata – Philippine violet
Chrysobalanus icaco – cocoplum
Clerodendrum – most species
Datura – devil's trumpet
Galphimia – thryallis
Hamelia patens – firebush
Hibiscus
Holmskioldia sanguinea –
   Chinese hat plant
Ixora
Jasminium – most species
Jatropha – most species
Justicia – most species
Malvaviscus arboreus – Turk's cap
Megaskepasma erythrochlamys –
   Brazillian red cloak

Odontonema strictum– firespike
Pachystachys lutea – golden shrimp
Plumbago
Pseuderanthemum laxiflorum –
   shooting star shrub
Rosa – rose
Russelia – firecracker plant
Ruttyruspolia – rutty
Tabernaemontana divaricata 'Flore
   Pleno' – crepe jasmine
Tabernaemontana divaricata 'Pinwheel'
   – pinwheel jasmine
Thunbergia erecta – king's mantle
Tibouchina urvilleana –
   princess flower

BIBLIOGRAPHY

Broschat, Timothy K., and Alan W. Meerow. *Betrock's Reference Guide to Florida Landscape Plants*. Gainesville, Florida: Betrock Information Systems, Inc., 1999.

Courtright, Gordon. *Tropicals*. Portland, Oregon: Timber Press, 1988.

Gilman, Edward F., and Robert J. Black. *Your Florida Guide to Shrubs*. Gainesville: University Press of Florida, 1999.

Graf, Alfred Byrd. *Tropica*. East Rutherford, New Jersey: Roehrs Company, 1981.

Liberty Hyde Bailey Hortorium. *Hortus Third*. New York: Macmillan Co., 1976.

Maxwell, Lewis S., and Betty M. Maxwell. *Florida Plant Selector*. Tampa, Florida: self-published, 1988.

Rauch, Fred D., and Paul R. Weissich. *Plants for Tropical Landscapes: A Gardener's Guide*. Honolulu: University of Hawaii Press, 2000.

Stresau, Frederic B. *Florida, My Eden*. Port Salerno, Florida: Florida Classics Library, 1986.

Western Garden Book. Menlo Park, California: Sunset Publishing Corporation, 2001.

Wyman, Donald. *Wyman's Gardening Encyclopedia*. New York: Macmillan Co., 1971.

INDEX

• Pages with illustrations are in italics
• Shrub listings in Classifications section (pp. 135-153) are not indexed here

157

black spot, 130, *130*
blue clerodendrum, *14*, 37, *38*
blue sage, *48*, 48
'Blush' loropetalum, 70
bog garden, 119, 131
bone meal, 118
botanical controls, 127
bougainvillea, *13*, *27*, 27, 114
Bougainvillea spectabilis, *13*, *27*, 27, *114*
Bougainvillea spectabilis 'Raspberry Ice', 27
border, shrub
    definition of, 13
    designing, 13
    examples of, *13*, 13
'Boxwood Beauty' natal plum, 33
Brazilian pepper tree, *16*, 16
Brazilian plume flower, 13, *66*, 66
Brazilian red cloak, *75*, 75
Breynia disticha, *28*, 28
Brugmansia, *13*, *29*, 29
Brunfelsia australis, 30
Brunfelsia pauciflora 'Floribunda', *30*, 30
Brunfelsia pauciflora 'Macrantha', 30
Brunfelsia pauciflora, 13, *30*, 30
buffer
    from salt spray, 118
    from wind, 113
'Burgundy' loropetalum, 70
bush allamanda, *24*, 24, *110*, *122*
bush clock vine, *105*, 105
butterflies, 127
butterfly garden
    definition of, 14
    examples of, *14*, 14
    insecticide use in, 127
    shrubs suitable for, 152–153
butterfly gardenia, 7, *101*, 101–102
buttonwood, *40*, 40

C

Caesalpinia pulcherrima, *31*, 31
calcium deficiency, 117
California
    climate of, 4, 114, 126
    diseases in, 126
    fertilizing in, 121, 122
    insects in, 126
    planting in, 118

    soil in, 114, 116, 118, 121
Calliandra emarginata, 32
Calliandra haematocephala 'Nana', 32
Calliandra haematocephala, 14, *15*, 15, *32*, 32
candle bush, 14, *97*, 97
cape honeysuckle, *104*, 104
cape jasmine, 7, *101*, *102*, 101–102
cardinal spear, *79*, 79
Caribbean, 4
caricature plant, *54*, 54
Carissa grandiflora 'Fancy', 33
Carissa grandiflora, *33*, 33
Carissa macrocarpa 'Boxwood Beauty', 33
Carissa macrocarpa 'Green Carpet', 33
Carissa macrocarpa 'Horizontalis', 33
Carissa macrocarpa 'Minima', 33
Carissa macrocarpa 'Prostrata', 33
Carissa macrocarpa 'Tuttle', 33
Carissa macrocarpa, 33
'Carnival' hibiscus, 56, *57*
cashmere bouquet clerodendrum, 37
cassava, variegated, *73*, 73
Cassia alata, 14, *97*, 97
Cassia bicapsularis, 14, *98*, 98
cassia, 14, 97–98
caterpillar, 127, 128, *128*
Cestrum aurantiacum, 34, 34
Cestrum nocturnum, *35*, 35
'Ceylon' copperleaf, *22*, 22
chartreuse shrimp plant, 65
chemical controls, 127
chemicals, combining, 132
chenille plant, *12*, 12, *21*, 21
China rose, 90, *91*
Chinese box, 10, 11, 15, *76*, 76
Chinese fringe, *70*, 70
Chinese hat plant, *58*, 58
Chinese silver privet, *69*, 69
Chinese witch hazel, *70*, 70
Chrysobalanus icaco 'Hobe Sound Dwarf', 36
Chrysobalanus icaco 'Red Tip', *36*, 36
Chrysobalanus icaco, 12, 15, *36*, 36
clay soil, 119
Clerodendrum bungei, 37
Clerodendrum minahassae, *37*, 37
Clerodendrum myricoides 'Ugandense', *14*,

dwarf ixora, 60, *61*
dwarf jatropha, 63
dwarf natal plum, 33
dwarf oleander, *78*, 78
dwarf peregrina, 63
'Dwarf Pink Mound' Singapore holly, *71*, 71
dwarf pittosporum, 81
dwarf poinciana, *31*, 31
dwarf powderpuff, 32
dwarf schefflera, *95*, 95
dwarf Singapore holly, *71*, 71
dwarf ti plant, 41

E
east exposure, 111
edibles, insect control for, 129
'Enchantress Pink' Indian hawthorn, 87
environmental stress
    aridity, 121
    drought, 120
    flooding, 120
    frost, 120, 122
    salinity, 117–118
    transplant shock, 118
Eranthemum pulchellum, *48*, 48
erosion, 120
'Escapade Blue' plumbago, 82
Eugenia uniflora, 10, *17*, *49*, 49
Euphorbia pulcherrima, *50*, 50
exposure, sun, 111

F
false aralia, *96*, 96, *129*
'Fancy' natal plum, 33
'Fascination' Indian hawthorn, 87
Feijoa sellowiana, *23*, 23
fertilizer
    burn, 121
    foliar, 121
    leaching of, 120
    manure, 117, 118, 119
    micronutrients, 120–121
    nitrogen, 121, 122, 123
    nutrients, types of, 116, 117, 118, 119, 120, 122, 123
    nutritional sprays, 121
    palm food, 121

    secondary elements, 120–121
    slow-release, 118, 121, 122
    trace elements, 121
fertilizing, 120–122
    acid-loving plants, 121
    arid soils, 121
    broadcasting, 121
    during frost, 122
    nutrient deficiencies, 116–117, *117*, *120*, 120, 121
    over-fertilizing, 121
    pH, 116–117
    planting, 118–119
    schedule, 120
firebush, 10, *55*, 55
firecracker plant, *92*, 92
'Fire Dragon' copperleaf, *22*, 22
firespike, *79*, 79
flame of the woods, 60
flamingo flower, 13, *66*, 66
'Flore Pleno' crepe jasmine, *101*, 101,
Florida
    climate of, 4, 114, 126
    diseases in, 126, 131
    fertilizing in, 120–122
    insects in, 126
    invasive plants in, 15–16
    planting in, 118
    soil in, 114, 116, 118, 120
flowering, 8, 112, 122,123, 124
focal point, 7
foliar fertilizer, 121
Fortuniana rootstock, 90
foundation planting
    description of, 8–9
    examples of, *8*, 9
    shrubs suitable for, 145–146
'Frasieri' Japanese privet, 69
fringed hibiscus, 56, *57*
frost, 3, 4, 122, 123, 125, 126
fungicide, 126, 127, 131, 132
Funginex, 131

G
Galphimia glauca, 51
Galphimia gracilus, 9, *51*, 51
Gardenia jasminoides 'Mystery', 52

160

dragonflies, *128*, 128
  ideal conditions for, 112, 117,
    125, 126–127
  ladybugs, *127*,
  leaf miners, 128
  leaf rollers, 128
  nematodes, harmful, 118, 120
  nocturnal, 128
  organic insecticides, 127, 128
  scale, 128–129, *129*
  toxic, 127, 128, 129
  whiteflies, 128–129
insecticides, 127, 128, 129
invasive plants
  definition of, 15–16
  examples of, *15,* 15, *16*, 16
  list of, 152
iron deficiencies, 116–117
irrigation, 117, 118, 119, 120, 121, 122
'Iwao Shimizu' ti plant, 41
Ixora 'Magee's Yellow', *61*
Ixora 'Maui', 60, *61*
Ixora 'Petite', 60, *61*
Ixora casei 'Super King', 60, 60
Ixora chinensis 'Nora Grant', 60
Ixora coccinea 'Flame of the Woods', 60
ixora, 60–61, 119, *120*, 121

J
'Jack Evans' Indian hawthorn, 87
'Jack Frost' Japanese privet, *69*, 69
'Jan Bier' croton, *39*
'Janet Craig' dracaena, 45
Japanese privet, *69*, 69
Japanese yew pine, *83*, 83
jasmine
  cape, 7, *101*, 101, *102*
  crepe, 7, *101*, 101, *102*
  downy, 14, *62*, 62
  night-blooming, *35*, 35
  orange, 10, 11, 15, *76*, 76
  pinwheel, 101, *102*
  shining, *14*, 14, *62*, 62
  star, 14, *62*, 62
Jasminium multiflorum, 12, 14, *62*, 62
Jasminium nitidum, *14*, 14, *62*, 62
Jatropha integerrima (*hastata*), *8*, *63*, 63
Jatropha integerrima 'Compacta', 63

Jatropha multifida, *64*, 64
'Java White' copperleaf, *22*, 22
Justicia betonica, *65*, 65
Justicia brandegeana, 9, *65*, 65
Justicia carnea, 13, *66*, 66

K
king's mantle, 10, *105*, 105
kurume azalea, *88*, 88

L
ladybugs, *127*, 127
Lagerstroemia speciosa, *67*, 67
Lagerstroemia, 67*, 67
lanai, shrubs suitable for, 150
landscape terms, 7
leaching, 9, 120
leadwort, *11*, *12*, *13*, *82*, 82
leaf burn, 132
leaf curl, 132
leaf miner insect, 128
leaf rollers, 128
leaf spots, 126, *130*, 130
Leucophyllum frutescens, *68*, 68
light
  decreasing, 112, 113
  excessive, 112
  exposure, 112–113
  microclimate, 112–113
  summer, 112
  winter, 112
Ligustrum japonicum 'Frasieri', 69
Ligustrum japonicum 'Howardi', 69
Ligustrum japonicum 'Jack Frost', *69*, 69
Ligustrum japonicum 'Rotundifolium', 69
Ligustrum japonicum, *69*, 69
Ligustrum sinense 'Variegatum', *69*, 69
liming, 116–117
lipstick hibiscus, *72*, 72
Loropetalum chinense 'Blush', 70
Loropetalum chinense 'Burgundy', 70
Loropetalum chinense 'Hines Purpleleaf', 70
Loropetalum chinense 'Monraz', 70
Loropetalum chinense, *70*, 70
loropetalum, *70*, 70
'Louise Phillipe' China rose, 90, *91*
love-lies-bleeding, *21*, 21

M

Madagascar rubber vine, *42*, 42
'Magee's Yellow' ixora, *61*, 61
maintainable height
    eight-foot shrubs, 140
    four-foot shrubs, 138–139
    pruning, 114–115
    six-foot shrubs, 139–140
    two-foot shrubs, 138
maintenance
    bank covers, 14
    fertilizing, 120–122
    foundation plantings, 8
    healthy plants, 126–127
    hedges, *11*, 11
    invasive plants, *15*, 15–16
    organic amendments, 117
    organic mulch, 117, 119, *120*,
        120
    plant selection, 113–114
    pruning, 9, 123–126
    size of plants, 113–114
magnesium, 116, 117
Malathion, 128, 132
Malaysia, 4
Malpighia coccigera, 71
Malpighia glabra, 71
Malpighia punica 'Dwarf Pink Mound',
    71, 71
Malpighia punica, *71*, 71
Malvaviscus arboreus, *72*, 72
'Mammey' croton, 39
manganese , 116, 117
Manihot esculenta 'Variegata', *73*, 73
manure, 117, 118, 119
mass plantings
    definitions of 12
    examples of, *12*, 13, 14
'Matensis' hibiscus, 56, *57*
mature height
    determining factors, 113–115
    medium shrubs, 136–137
    small shrubs, 136
    tall shrubs, 137–138
Maui, 60, *61*
Medinilla magnifica, 74
Medinilla myriantha, *17*, *74*, 74, 133
medinilla*, 17*, *74*, 74

Mediterranean, 4
Megaskepasma erythrochlamys, *75*, 75
Mexican rose, *44*, 44
microbial products, 127
microclimate, 112–113
micronutrients, 120, 121, 122
microorganisms, 116, 118, 120
mildew, 130
mineral controls, 127, 131
miniature holly, *71*, 71
miniature rose, 90, *91*
'Minima' natal plum, 33
mirror-leafed viburnum, *10*, 10, 107
'Miss Aceton' croton, *39*
mold, 130
'Monraz' loropetalum, 70
'Mr. Lincoln' hybrid tea rose, 90
'Mrs. B. R. Cant' tea rose, 90, *91*
mulch, 112, 117, 118, 119, *120*, 120
Murraya paniculata, 10, 11, 15, *76*, 76
Mussaenda erythrophylla, *77*, 77
Mussaenda incana, *77*, 77
Mussaenda philippica, *77*, 77
mussaenda, *77*, 77
'Musaica' copperleaf, *22*, 22
mystery gardenia, 52

N

'Nana' holly, *59,* 59
nasturtium bauhinia, *26*, 26
natal plum, *33*, 33, 36, 136
native habitat, 111
nematodes, harmful, 118, 120
Nerium oleander 'Petite Pink', 78,
Nerium oleander 'Petite Salmon', *78*, 78
Nerium oleander, 78, 78, 113, 116
neutral soil pH, 116
New Zealand, 4
night-blooming jasmine, *35*, 35
nitrogen, 121, 122, 123
nocturnal insects, 128
nodes, 126
non-native plants, 116, 118, 119
'Nora Grant' ixora, 60
north exposure, 111
nutrient deficiencies, 116–117, *117*, 120
nutrient toxicity, 117
nutrients *(see* fertilizing)

ribbon plant, 45, *45*, 136
rock, planting in, 118, 119
roots, 113, 118
Rosa 'Don Juan', 90, *91*
Rosa 'Louise Phillipe', 90, *91*
Rosa 'Mr. Lincoln', 90
Rosa 'Mrs. B. R. Cant', 90, *91*
Rosa 'Old Blush', 90, *91*
Rosa 'Red Cascade', 90, *91*
Rosa 'Tropicana', 90, *91*
Rosa, 90–91
rose, 90–91, *129*
'Rosemount' hydrangea tree, *44*, 44
rot, 126, 130
'Rotundifolium' Japanese privet, 69
'Royal Cape' plumbago, 82
rubber vine, *42*, 42
Russelia equisetiformis, *92*, 92
rusts, 131
rutty, 8, *93*, 93
Ruttyruspolia 'Phyllis Van Heeden', 8, *93*, 93

S
Safer's Insecticidal Soap, 128
salinity, 113, 117–118
salt tolerance, 151–152
Sanchezia speciosa, *94*, 94
'Sandankwa' viburnum, 10, *107*, 107
scale insects, 128–129, *129*
scarlet bush, 10, *55*, 55
'Scarletta' hibiscus, *57*
Schefflera actinophylla, *15*, 15
Schefflera arboricola 'Trinette', *95*, 95
Schefflera arboricola, *95*, 95
Schefflera elegantissima, *1*, *96*, 96
Schillings holly, *11*, 59
Schinus terebinthifolius, *16*, 16
screens
    definition of, 10
    examples of, *10*, 10
    microclimates, 113
    shrubs suitable for, 146
    vertical elements, 113
secondary elements, 120, 121, 122
Senna alata, *97*, 97
Senna bicapsularis, *98*, 98
Senna, 14

Sevin, 128
shade
    decreasing, 112–113
    east exposure, 111
    excessive, 112
    microclimate, 112–113
    north exposure, 111
    partial, *111*, 111
    producing, 113
seasonal, 112
shining jasmine, *14*, 14, *62*, 62
shooting star clerodendrum, 37, *38*
shooting star shrub, *85*, 85
shower-of-gold thryallis, 51
shrimp plant, 9, *65*, 65, *80*, 80
shrub
    definition of, 3
    training as a tree, 3
shrub border
    definition of, 13
    examples of, 13, *13*
shrub encyclopedia, 135–153
silver buttonwood, *40*, 40
'Silver Dwarf Discovery' allamanda, *24*, 24, *122*
'Silver Sheen' buttonwood, 40
silverleaf, *68*, 68
Singapore holly, *71*, 71
size of plants, 113–114
    factors determining, 114
    foundation plantings, 9
    immature heights, 113
    maintainable heights, 114
    mature heights, 114
sky flower, *47*, 47
slow-release fertilizer, 118, 121, 122
snowbush, *28*, 28
soap, insecticidal, 128
soil, 116–117, 118, 120,130
    acidic, 116, 119
    alkaline, 9, 116–117, 119
    arid, 17, 117–118, 120, 121
    clay, 119
    compacted, 119
    drainage, 17, 119–120, 130
    erosion, 120
    in Arizona, 114, 116, 118, 121
    in California, 114, 116, 118, 121

in Florida, 114, 116, 118, 120
in Hawaii, 114, 117, 119
liming of, 116
neutral, 116
nutrient deficiencies in,
    116–117, *117*, 120
nutrient toxicity of, 117
pH, 116–117, 118
planting in, 118–119
saline, 117–118, 120, 121
sandy, 118, 119
sulfur in, 117
sweet, 9, 116–117, 119
testing of, 116
wet, 151
solarium, 4
song-of-India, 45, *46*
sooty mold, *130*, 130
South Africa, 4
South America, 4
south exposure, 111
South Pacific, 4
Southern California, 4
southern Indian azalea, *88*, 88
species, 115
specimen
    definition of, 7
    examples of, 7
    shrubs suitable for, 143–144
'Springtime' Indian hawthorn, 87
star jasmine, 14, *62*, 62
stem, 3
'Stokes Dwarf' holly, 59
Strelitzia nicolai, 99, *99*
Strelitzia reginae, 99, *99*, 100
stress (*see* environmental stress)
subtropics, 4
sulfur, 117
sulfur fungicide, 127, 131
summer poinsettia, 77, 77
sun
    decreasing, 112, 113
    excessive, 112
    exposure, 111–112
    flowering in, 14, 123
    microclimate, 112–113
    promoting, *112*, 112, 113
    shrubs suitable for, 141–142

summer, 112
winter, 112
'Super King' ixora, *60*, 60
Surinam cherry, 10, *17*, *49*, 49
sweet soil, 116–117
sweet viburnum, *10*, 10, 107
systemic insecticides, 128, 129

T

Tabernaemontana divaricata 'Flore
    Pleno', 7, *101*, 101, *102*
Tabernaemontana divaricata 'Pinwheel', 101,
    102
Tabernaemontana divaricata, 7, 101–102
Tahitian gardenia, *52*, 52
tapioca, variegated, *73*, 73
taxonomy
    definition of, 115–116
    genus, 115
    hybridization, 115
    species, 115
    variety, 115
tea rose, 90, *91*
Tecoma stans, *103*, 103
Tecomaria capensis 'Aurea', *104*, 104
Tecomaria capensis, *104*, 104
Texas sage, *68*, 68
Texas, 4
thorny plants, 9
thryallis, 9, *51*, 51
Thunbergia erecta 'Alba', 105
Thunbergia erecta, 10, *105*, 105
thunbergia gardenia, *8*, 52
Thuricide, 127
ti plant, *8*, *41*, 41
Tibouchina urvilleana, *106*, 106
toadstools, 126
topiary, *17*
toxic chemicals, 127, 128, 129
toxicity, nutrient, 117
trace elements, 121, 122
transplant shock, 118
tree hibiscus, *56*, 56
trees
    shrubs suitable as, 148
    training into shrubs, 3
tricolor dracaena, *45*, 45
Tropic of Cancer, 3

If you enjoyed reading this book, here are some other books from Pineapple Press on related topics. For a complete catalog, write to Pineapple Press, P.O. Box 3889, Sarasota, Florida 34230, or call (800) 746-3275. Or visit our website at www.pineapplepress.com.

The Art of South Florida Gardening by Harold Songdahl and Coralee Leon. Gardening advice specifically written for the unique conditions of south Florida. This practical, comprehensive guide, written with humor and know-how, will teach you how to outsmart the soil, protect against pests and weather, and select the right trees and shrubs for Florida's climate. ISBN 1-56164-088-3 (pb)

Flowering Trees of Florida by Mark Stebbins. If you just can't get enough of majestic trees and brightly colored flowers, you'll love this book. Written for both the seasoned arborist and the weekend gardener alike, this comprehensive guide offers 74 outstanding tropical flowering trees that will grow in Florida's subtropical climate. Full-color photos throughout. ISBN 1-56164-173-1 (pb)

Gardening in the Coastal South by Marie Harrison. A Master Gardener discusses coastal gardening considerations such as salt tolerance; environmental issues such as pesticide use, beneficial insects, and exotic invasives; and specific issues such as gardening for butterflies and birds. Color photos and charming pen-and-ink illustrations round out the text, which covers perennials, herbs, shrubs and small trees, vines, and edible flowers. ISBN 1-56164-274-6 (pb)

Key West Gardens and Their Stories by Janis Frawley-Holler. Venture off the beaten track and get a rare glimpse into the lushly green and flowered gardens of old Key West. Enjoy beautiful views of the islanders' sanctuaries as well as fascinating stories and histories of the grounds where gardens now grow. More than 170 gorgeous color photos accompany the text. ISBN 1-56164-204-5 (pb)

Guide to the Gardens of Florida by Lilly Pinkas. This comprehensive guide to Florida's gardens includes detailed information about featured species and garden facilities as well as directions, hours of operation, and admission fees. Learn the history and unique offerings of each garden, what plants to see and the best time of year to see them. Traveling outside of Florida? Check out *Guide to the Gardens of Georgia* and *Guide to the Gardens of South Carolina* by the same author. **Florida** ISBN 1-56164-169-3 (pb); **Georgia** ISBN 1-56164-198-7 (pb); **South Carolina** ISBN 1-56164-251-7 (pb)

Exotic Foods: A Kitchen and Garden Guide by Marian Van Atta. Take advantage of year-round warm weather and grow fruit trees, exotic vegetables, and rare delights such as Surinam cherry. Discover tips to keep your garden free of pests and producing for years. Includes a wealth of delicious and nutritious recipes for drinks, main courses, desserts, relishes, jams, and jellies. ISBN 1-56164-215-0 (pb)